JN418916

The Miracle of Absolute Positivity

Positivity
Positivity
Positivity
Positivity
Positivity
Positivity

The Miracle of Absolute Positivity

Younghoon Lee

CGW | LOGOS USA

Conte

nts

Conte

nts

Conte

nts

Prologue

When God does what humans cannot, we call that a miracle. Our very existence is a miracle in itself. In the year 2022 alone, 70 million people have died due to various reasons such as COVID-19, diseases, old age, war, accidents, drug overdose, and mental illnesses. It's an average of 180,000 deaths per day. But God has given us today as a gift. It is because God wants to carry out His will through us. If we wake up this morning, still breathing, our hearts still pumping, it still means that we have a calling to live for. To carry out God's calling in our lives, we must make this one and only life of value. This is carrying out the calling.

My spiritual mentor Rev. Yong-gi Cho has taught me to be filled with the Holy Spirit and possess the faith of absolute positivity. Ever since, I have experienced many amazing miracles that has come from the faith of absolute positivity. God is the God of absolute positivity and when we meet Him all negativity vanishes from our lives. The Miracle of Fivefold Positivity occurs with our view of myself, view of others, view of work and calling, environment, and future becoming renewed.

However, to experience this Fivefold Positivity, we must train ourselves with these three things, positive language, absolute gratitude, and sharing our love for others. When we understand the principles of absolute positivity, train ourselves, and apply them in our lives, we will live a life of miracles pleasing the Lord and completing our calling.

This book explains the importance of absolute positivity, and fundamental principles and examples. At the end of each chapter, a Check List of 10 items is included. I personally think that Positivity Quotient is more important than Intelligent Quotient and Emotional Quotient. When the Positivity Quotient increases the degree of happiness and fulfillment of our life, faith increases as well.

Also, the 4th Dimension Absolute Positivity Workbook has been published. The workbook includes Bible studies under different topics as well as meditation and application for small groups supplementing this current book. May your faith be more determined in our absolutely positive God as you interact with this book. As you learn and apply the Fivefold Positivity and Threefold Training, may all your negativity be transformed into positivity which is the miracle of God's love.

Now are you ready to embark on this miraculous journey of absolute positivity with me?

Rev. Dr. **Younghoon Lee**
Senior Pastor of Yoido Full Gospel Church

The Miracle of Absolute Positivity

Above all else, guard your heart,
for everything you do flows from it.

Proverbs 4:23

Chapter 01

The Importance of Absolute Positivity

Chapter **01**

The Importance of Absolute Positivity

> Attitude is an outward look on our past experiences.
> It is the prophet of our future.
>
> **-John Maxwell**

There was a time I had dinner with a retired doctor, he was 83 years of age. However, his age did not limit him from maintaining an active life even enjoying a social life. I was interested in how he was able to come to that point. Surprisingly, he explained to me that he himself battled illnesses while taking care of others who were ill. The reason he was able to maintain a healthy and active life was that he continued to think thoughts of gratitude and proclaimed in words that he was thankful. His pain disappeared as he kept saying, "I'm thankful, I'm thankful." Here's what he shared. "Rev. Lee, I don't listen to negative news or gossips of any kind. I completely block myself from them. I only focus on positive thoughts, so I am at peace." Through his testimony, I was reminded once again of the power of absolute positive thoughts and confessions of gratitude.

Positive people are healthy

People today are most conscious of their health. They invest a lot of time and money in new vitamins, healthy foods, and exercises. They share the newest trends with one another on health and wellness. However, doctors say the most important thing in health care is stress management. You can't maintain a peace of mind when you carry anxiety and hurt. Ultimately, negative thoughts keep us from having a peace of mind.

In Korea, on average approximately 10,000 people commit suicide and 100,000 attempt suicide annually. According to Statistics Korea, suicide was the leading cause of death among teenagers at 43.7%. It's also estimated that 2.5 to 3 million people are prescribed for anxiety disorders annually.

Dr. Emerson of the U.S. National Health Service conducted an experiment to find out the relationship between gratitude and health.

He divided the participants into three groups: A, B, and C. Group A had unpleasant words and actions, Group B had daily words and actions, and Group C had positive words and actions reflecting gratitude. After a set period of time, he analyzed the changes in the health status of the participants in each group. It was confirmed that the health status and happiness level of the participants in Group C who positively gave thanks were the highest. Through this study, Dr. Emerson concluded that the frequent use of positive language and words of gratitude increases immunity, overcoming large and small diseases and living a much healthier life.

Dr. John Henry Jowett, announced in a report after studying "People with gratitude who pray before their meals" have three unique substances found in them. He said, "Gratitude is a vaccine, an antitoxin, and an antiseptic." What did he mean? He meant that gratitude, like a vaccine, can prevent the invasion of a disgruntled, discouraged spirit. Like an antitoxin, gratitude can prevent the effects of the poisons of cynicism, criticalness, and grumbling. Like an antiseptic, a spirit of gratitude can soothe and heal the most troubled spirit.

Harold Koenig and David B. Larson, M.D. of Duke University Medical Center conducted an experimental study, which found that people who attend church weekly, worshipping with gratitude, live an average of 7 years longer than those who do not. In addition, Dr. John Henry Jowett explained that "Gratitude is a vaccine, an antitoxin, and an antiseptic."

Stress is known to be the cause of many diseases. Negative emotions such as intense hatred and fury, depression and frustration are stressful. When stressed, the body releases stress hormones, displaying symptoms such as throbbing of the heart and headaches. Furthermore, it destroys nutrients such as vitamins that are vital for the human body. It also suppresses the immune system. Stress causes diseases in the cardiovascular, circulatory, and digestive system, etc.

While praying into the New Year, God told me this. "I will give you greater grace in the future, no matter what, don't let your peace of mind be taken away." Upon hearing this, I was determined. "Yes, I'll fix my eyes on the Lord and hold on fast to His words of promise. Under any circumstance, if we trust Him, He will give us peace. So, let's not lose this peace. Let's not be swayed by words of people or the environment."

The Lord has already promised to give his peace as a gift. "Peace I leave with you; my peace I give you. I do not give to you as the world gives. Do not let your hearts be troubled and do not be afraid." John 14:27 All trouble and pain originate from your heart. If we can guard our heart and thoughts, we can win in every situation Proverbs 4:23.

In fact, people who think of themselves negatively, about the environment, about others, those having a negative outlook are vulnerable to mental illness and stress. However, if we have positive thoughts and gratitude, we can overcome hurts and stress and take good care of our health. Dr. Irving Oil explains, "Positive mindsets and beautiful thoughts produce hormones that are valuable to the body and can be helpful in curing diseases." These findings clearly show that positive thoughts can protect the mind as well as the body's health.

Positivity creates happiness

Among the graduates from Mills College, California, a study was conducted analyzing 141 yearbook photos from the graduating class of 1960. Some of the graduates were expressionless, but most of the others were smiling. But half of them were smiling only with their facial expressions, and the other half were smiling with a smile from the heart. Two psychologists monitored the students' lives.

They visited women who were 27, 43, and 52 years old among the graduates and examined the satisfaction of their life and marriage. As shown by the results, the people who really smiled were living happier. These women who genuinely smiledDuchenne showed a high sense of accomplishment, a good interpersonal relationship, a stable psychological state, and a high level of personal income.

People usually think that certain conditions must be met for happiness to occur, such as, "If you make a lot of money," "If you have a great job," "If you become healthy," and "If your children go to a good school". However, Sonja Lyubomirsky, a psychology professor in America who had been doing research on Positive Psychology, says wealth and success are not conditions for happiness, but rather, a result of happiness. She said, "What brings happiness is a positive attitude to life, and people who are happy because of it are more productive, have a healthy immune system and make more money." Positive thoughts about yourself and positive attitude towards the environment and the future determine your life.

Life is a battle between a positive image and a negative image

Life is a battle between positivity and negativity. The human mind is a battlefield of positivity and negativity. Proverbs 4:23 testifies, "Above all else, guard your heart, for everything you do flows from it."

What you see depends on your mind. Even if you look at the same thing at the same time, at the same place, everything looks different depending on your mindset and interests. When looking at the reservoir, a swimmer imagines swimming, the fisherman dreams of catching a big fish, a farmer imagines a scene of a well-watered field and harvesting abundant fruit, while a person who enjoys water sports imagines making waves riding a beautiful boat. This is how important one's perspective, and mindset is.

Thomas J. Stanley wrote a book called *The Millionaire Minds* after conducting surveys and interviews with 733 millionaires. In the book, he says, "Many millionaires aren't highly educated elites, nor were they people who inherited a huge wealth. They are people who have a millionaire's dream and are armed with a millionaire's mind." As the book says, depending on how you set your mind, your words, and facial expressions change. You would dress differently, and your behavior would change. Depending on your mindset, your faith and life changes. Therefore, we must dream and visualize our image of happiness and success. We must create positive images every day.

Ms. Kelly Choi ran a business in Paris and failed, accruing a debt of one million dollars. However, she wasn't disheartened, but rather, she met with 1000 people who accumulated great wealth and studied the principles of wealth and success. As a result, she formed a global company called 'KellyDeli,' expanding to 1,200 stores in 12 European countries and achieving annual sales of 600 billion KRW. In her best-selling book, *Wealthinking*, Kelly Choi presents the concept of what healthy wealth looks like and highlights the key elements of success.

> *If you ask what the key components of my success were, I wouldn't hesitate to tell you "To meditate and visualize." Visualization is the main essence of Wealthinking. Visualization is to dream and visualize my desired life and to meditate them in my subconscious mind.*

The most important thing in life's success is how to picture an image. The same goes for an athletes' success. They have trained for a long time understanding the importance of image training. This is crucial in a successful performance of an athletes. Athletes routinely use visualization techniques as part of their training, imaging themselves performing a certain skill confidently or winning in an upcoming game. On a similar principle, an experiment was conducted in which people who never bowled before were divided into two groups and were taught how to bowl. Videos were recorded of both groups practicing, showing only the good scenes in one group, and the bad scenes in the other. As a result, one group's skills improved significantly after seeing them bowl well. In addition, the bowling skills improved for the group who didn't bowl well after watching positive performances.

Heung-min Son is a world-class soccer player born in Korea. In an interview with Singapore's media *AUGUSTMAN* after the 2022 Qatar World Cup, he expressed his feelings.

> *Positive thinking is important. When I suffered a facial fracture just before the World Cup, people said, "Heung-min Son's World Cup is gone." "But I thought positively. I was sure I would go to the World Cup."*

From the words above, you can feel the strong positivity of

Heung-min Son. It is very important to picture a positive image even in this type of difficult situation.

Fred Polak, a Dutch futurologist talked about the importance of images. "The rise and fall of images of the future precedes or accompanies the rise and fall of cultures. As long as a society's image is positive and flourishing, the flower of culture is in full bloom. Once the image begins to decay and lose its vitality, the culture does not long survive."

What images are you picturing? What image do you have of yourself, of others, of your work? What image do you have about your problems, or about your family, church, company, or society? Is the picture positive? Or is it negative? Obviously, positive thoughts bring an image of positivity and negative thoughts bring an image of negativity. Also, depending on the image, your future can change.

Surround yourself with people who have positive energy

Conformity is the energy that causes waves to react to other objects. If you adjust the violin string to the same pitch and play on one line, the other string will make the same sound as well. Human emotions can also have a similar phenomenon. When someone next to you is depressed, you may feel a little bit down too, and when someone is bright and happy, you may feel the same as well. The same goes for negative energy. If someone thinks negatively and speaks negatively, it can be contagious to others who are around. Therefore, we should be the ones who initiate a positive community by sending positive vibes and energy through the effects of conformity.

The best way to strengthen one's positive image is to be with someone who has positive energy. John Gordon, a positive energy expert and best-selling author, is spreading positive energy throughout the United States with a program called 'PEP Positive Energy Program.' His book called *Energy Bus* introduces the secret to developing positive energy. It is to surround yourself with positive people, put them on the energy bus, and run together towards the purpose of your life. He emphasizes not to hang out with negative people because it's wasting your energy on those who are draining your positive energy. You should surround yourself with positive people that leads to more meaningful and beautiful things in life.

Tom Peters, who is a business management pioneer gives this

crucial advice. He says, "Give positive feedback to your team members." He shares that giving positive attention is 30 times more powerful than negative attention in creating high performance on a team. Even Jesus said when the word of God is planted on good soil, seeds grow to its fruition even to thirty times Mark 4:20. A positive heart is the good soil that receives and embraces the word of God with sincerity. With a positive mind and speech, you may achieve positive effects even to 30 times or more.

Sociologist Cumming Walk says there are four components of success. The first is intelligence IQ, the second is knowledge, the third is technique, and the fourth is attitude. Among them, he said, "positive attitude" plays more than 93% of the importance in determining success. Positive attitudes have a profound impact on interpersonal relationships and success in life. There isn't anything you can't do if you are connected with positive people with positive energy. You have unlimited possibilities. We also must ride the positive energy bus with absolute positivity as we go forward with the dreams and visions that God leads us to.

Even 1,330 mistakes can be seen with positivity

On our way towards God's dreams, we experience mistakes

and failures. Difficult times may come. However, when we have the peace of mind with absolute positivity, we can overcome any feelings of despair.

Babe Ruth is a one of the most famous baseball players in American baseball history. He hit 714 home runs, maintaining the world record until 1976. Babe Ruth's "Called Shot" which he directed his bat before hitting the homerun ball, has been a regular theme in movies and stories. However, while many people know that Babe Ruth is the home run king, not many know that he is the record holder for strikeouts.

He has struck out 1,330 times, and many experts say that this record is as hard as his homerun record. He said he needed 1,330 strikeouts to hit 714 home runs. In the end, 1,330 mistakes made him the greatest baseball player in Major League history. People who are afraid of mistakes or failures cannot maximize their potentials. This is why we must have absolute positivity even amid mistakes or failures in life.

It is not the wind that determines the direction of the ship, but the sail of the boat. The direction in which the sail is directed determines the ship's direction. Also, how high a balloon can fly depends not on the color of the balloon or the direction of the wind, but on what is inside of the balloon. Likewise, our thoughts in our minds may determine the direction and height of life.

This next example is how Alexander Fleming discovered penicillin. At the time, he was experimenting with the influenza virus that was common among the children. Fleming returned from a holiday, to find mold growing on a Petri dish of Staphylococcus bacteria. He had accidently left the lid open. Fleming wasn't disappointed nor did he give up. Upon examination of the mold, he noticed that the culture was preventing the growth of the bacteria. It produced a self-defense chemical that killed the bacteria. He investigated the Petri dishes and in so doing, discovered the antibiotic penicillin, winning him a Nobel Prize in Medicine. His positive and resilient attitude towards his lab mistake led him to the newfound path of success.

In America, a certain Christian man had spent a lifetime filled with failures and despair rather than happiness. His business venture failed at age 22, he failed in the state elections at age 23, he failed again in business at age 24. He was elected to state legislature at 25, the woman he loved died when he was 26. At age 27, he had a nervous breakdown and schizophrenia, he ran for Congress at 29, lost the presidency at 31, lost the House of Representatives at 34, at age 37 he was barely elected as a Representative to lose it 2 years later. That isn't the end, at age 46 he lost the Senate race, at age 47 he lost the bid for Vice Presidency, and at the age of 49 he lost the Senate race again. Then, at the age of 51, he was elected the 16th President of the United States.

His name is Abraham Lincoln. He became God's great servant who laid a great foundation for the establishment of true human rights and peace in America. He ended slavery and created the possibility of civil and social freedom for African Americans. His life seemed to be a series of failures and discouragements, however, without despair he moved forward with the faith of absolute positivity. God accomplished many great things through him.

No matter what others say, remember of Jonah

An inventor that all of us know, Thomas Edison, was a positive person. However, when we look at his past, he had many unfortunate events. At an early age, he used to sell newspapers on the railroad. In the baggage car, he used to set up a laboratory for his chemistry experiments. One day an accidental fire from his experiment broke out and led to the train conductor tossing him out and Edison being hit on the ears in the process. As a result, he lost almost all his hearing. His disability could have become the obstacle for his future as an inventor but when someone asked of the influence of his disability he said, "This is a blessing, because it helped him to avoid useless distractions when reading and experimenting."

On February 8, 1947, an event was held to celebrate the 100th year of Edison's birth. During the event, people found a tightly closed drawer as they were looking through Edison's room and his memorabilia. People wondered what could've been inside, closed for 100 years. So, they opened the drawer by force. Surprisingly, there was a piece of paper that said, "When down in the mouth remember Jonah. He came out all right."

The prophet Jonah went against God's command and fled from Him. He then was tossed into the sea and was swallowed by a fishJonah 1:17. But God protected him and appointed the fish vomit him out at Nineveh where Jonah was supposed to go toJonah 2:1-10. Now we must remember that God worked and saved Nineveh even through Jonah, who was disobedient and stubborn. Perhaps Edison wrote this note as a reminder to live with faith of absolute positivity.

"When down in the mouth remember Jonah." Let us be encouraged through Jonah. Even when our life seems difficult and tiring, if we have an attitude of absolute positivity and faith, our lives can be restored.

A positive person is highly resilient

A person with positive thoughts can overcome any adversity. 'Resiliency' describes our ability to cope with difficult situations. The term is used in various fields such as psychology, sociology, economics, and pedagogy.

Since 1955, researchers Emmy E. Werner and Ruth S. Smith in their seminal study of risk and resilience, followed nearly 833 children born in impoverished conditions in Kauai on Hawaii's islands for more than 30 years. Werner and Smith found that approximately two-thirds of the children who grew up in impoverished conditions experienced a wide variety of negative situations such as delinquency in education, substance abuse, and social conflicts. However, 72 out of 201 in the high-risk group matured into competent, caring, responsible citizens. They examined the one-third of the high-risk sample that managed to excel and determined that these individuals shared factors, such as positive energy which likely led to resilience.

The children who did not develop problems despite risk and adversity and adjusted successfully with positive energy were called "Resilient." As there is elasticity in every object, it has been found that people have the resiliency of life as well when they are faced with the most persistent adverse circumstances.

Professor Warner's team said that there are three factors to resilience: self-regulation, interpersonal skills, and positivity. The most important among the three is positivity. Strengthening positivity can increase self-regulation and interpersonal skills at the same time, and when it becomes a habit, it can increase resilience.

Resilience is when an individual or community that has experienced adversity or unhappiness has the power to recover and find its place or climb higher without being discouraged. The works of children fairy tale writer Hans Christian Andersen show examples of resilience. He was born into a very poor family and did not receive a proper education, however, he sublimated *The Matchbox Girl*, and amid a broken heart, he created the masterpiece, *The Little Mermaid.* In addition, from the experience of being teased for his ugly appearance, the *Ugly Duckling* was born. He couldn't avoid the adversity and challenges that came into his life, but he overcame them and made a great leap forward. What came to be a stumbling block was turned into a steppingstone. A positive person can fulfill God's dream by sublimating any hardships in life.

Increase your Positivity Quotient(PQ)

Just as each person has an Intelligence Quotient IQ different from their Emotional Quotient EQ, the Positivity Quotient PQ is also different. Increasing an individual's positive index creates meaningful changes in his or her life and faith, and increasing the positive index of the community allows the community to be renewed and achieve its major goals. I first talked about the changes that the principle of absolute positivity brings in life. Next, I'll talk about how to self-evaluate and raise your positivity index. First, I would like to share the Fivefold positivity based on the belief of having absolute positivity towards God.

The most important thing here is being positive about yourself. Every thought begins with oneself. If we don't affirm ourselves first, we can't correctly affirm others or the community. Second, is being positive to others. The Bible says, "Let's respect each other first." Romans 12:10 The basis of a successful interpersonal relationship is respect and positivity to the other person. Third, is being positive about work. There should be a sense of responsibility and positivity for what I do. When I have a positive attitude about what I do at home, at work, or at church, joy will come, and I can perform well. Fourth, is being positive about the environment. In life, we encounter problems big and small and face difficulties. Our attitude towards the problem is important. When people of faith were met with a problem, they had victory through faith by looking towards a God who is greater than the problem. In addition, positive thoughts about the community I belong to is important. The positivity I have towards the church or company I belong to has a great influence on my faith, work, and happiness. The last is positivity towards the future. Life comes true as you dream and see it. You must have that kind of expectation of the future. If you carry God's dream and move forward with faith, good things will surely happen.

To be equipped with the Fivefold positivity, the Threefold training is important. First, proclamation of positive language and training is important. Proclaim positive language for yourself, others, what you do, the environment, and the future, then you and your community will experience amazing changes. Second, absolute gratitude training is important. Whatever you do, it's necessary to confess your gratitude with thanksgiving. For a person who gives thanks daily, he or she will experience the miracle of a God who supplies. Third, we need to train in sharing love with others. Those who are depressed, those who cause problems, focus only on their inner self or their emotions. Such people are more likely to be unhappy. However, if you start sharing love with others, you can become a positive person and in turn a positive person can share more love.

The source of the Fivefold positivity and Threefold training rests on the person's positivity towards God. A person who has positivity towards God can be positive in all things. God is the God of absolute positivity. Everyone who trusts and follows God can receive from the stream of absolute positivity for the fountain of positivity never runs dry.

Absolute Positivity Diagram

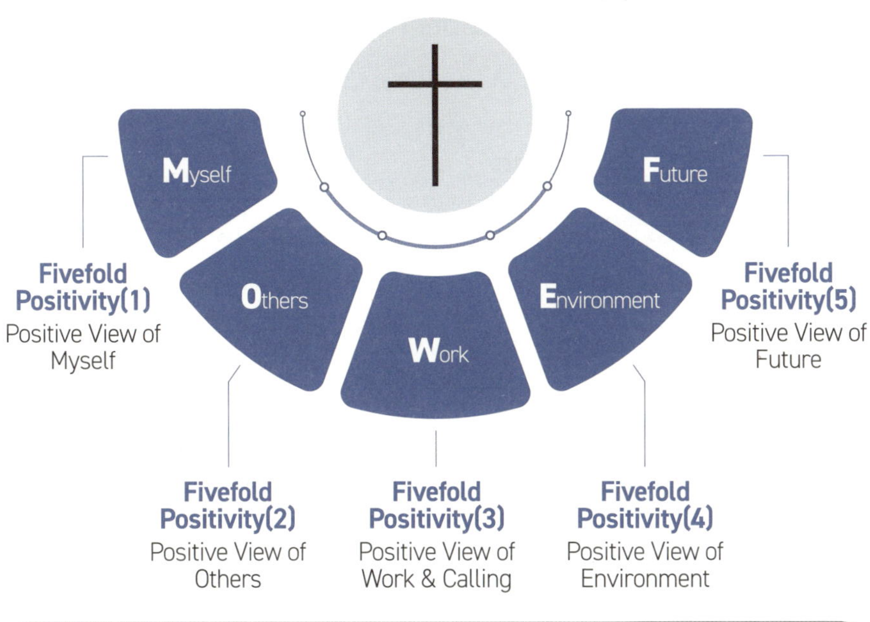

Fivefold Positivity and Threefold Training(MOWEF PTS)

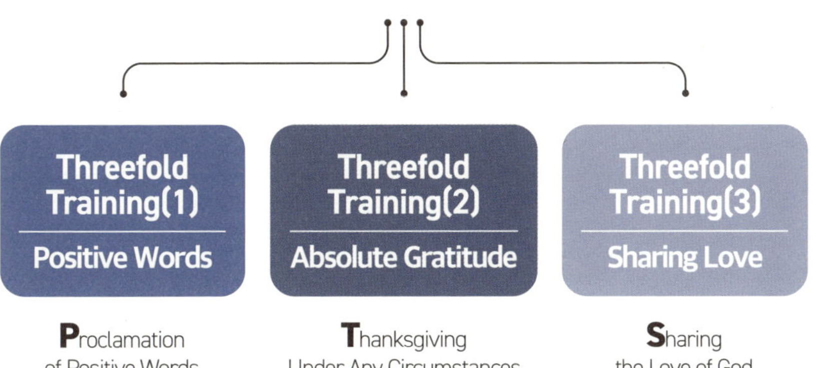

Positivity Quotient Check List ☑

Positive Attitude Quotient Check List?

Instructions: Please read each statement and select the most appropriate response to indicate how frequently you experience the behavior described in the statement.

Statements	Never	Rarely	Some times	Often	Always
	1	2	3	4	5
1. When stressed, I think positively and overcome it.					
2. Negative emotions don't determine the attitude or direction of life.					
3. After experiencing hardship and difficulty, I learn from them and get back up.					
4. I usually believe in the power of positivity and am very conscious about it.					
5. I have high expectations of my remaining life and future.					
6. When looking at the environment or people, I try to see the brighter side than the darker.					
7. I visualize myself doing well or succeeding.					
8. There are more people who say positive things around me than negative things.					
9. I don't think I'm going to fail at something before I start it.					
10. I have a lot of love and positive energy in me.					

After reading each statement, check the corresponding box.
Add up the checked scores for each statement.

Totals (   ) points

The Miracle of Absolute Positivity

And we know that in all things
God works for the good of those who love him,
who have been called according to his purpose.

Romans 8:28

Chapter 02

Positivity towards God of Absolute Positivity

Chapter **02**

Positivity towards God of Absolute Positivity

> Never say the word impossible
> Just throw it away in the trash.
>
> **– Goethe**

I learned the importance of being filled with the Holy Spirit and absolute positivity from my spiritual mentor Rev. Yong-gi Cho. Rev. Yong-gi Cho always desired to be filled with the Holy Spirit, prayed passionately and approached the word of God with faith of absolute positivity. As these two have become important pillars of my life and faith, I have always tried to balance them. This is because I've experienced being filled with the Holy Spirit and absolute positivity, they go together. I can do well in whatever that I've been charged with.

Absolute positivity enjoyed through the goodness of God

The first thing to know is that God is the God of absolute positivity. Our God, who is always positive, is always a good God. Christian faith begins with faith in a good God. God created heaven, earth and man and said it was very good to see. "God saw all that he had made, and it was very good"Genesis 1:31. Although man became corrupt by the sins of pride and disobedience, God loved man and the world he created, so he decided to create us new in ChristEphesians 1:4.

Christian faith is absolute positivity centered on the word of God and the cross of Jesus. If you look into the gospel of Jesus Christ, there is no negative factor to be found anywhere. The gospel of the cross is complete and full. The full gospel is a message of absolute positivity for us all. God wants us to enjoy good health and that all may go well with us, even as our soul is getting along well3 John 1:2. God loves us so much, He wanted to give the most joyful and blessed news, the gospel to all mankind through the cross of Jesus Christ. If you believe in Jesus, you will be saved and will gain eternal lifeGospel of Regeneration, be filled with the Spirit of the LordGospel of the Fullness of the Holy Spirit, restored and healed holistically in body, soul, and spiritGospel of Divine Healing, blessed under all circumstancesGospel of Blessing, after the second coming of Jesus, believers with heavenly hope will enter heavenGospel of the Second Coming, this good news has been given to us.

We must hold on to the Fivefold gospel that has been presented to us through the cross. We must fight the thoughts of discouragement and despair. God is good, God is great, God is faithful, God is love and we must look to Him and move forward with faith of absolute positivity. One of my favorite Bible verses is Romans 8:28. This verse contains God's absolute sovereignty and all things come together for good, the message of absolute positivity.

> *We know that in all things God works for the good of those who love him, who have been called according to his purpose.*
> *_ Romans 8:28*

Absolute positivity within God's sovereign love

The main character of the Bible is Jesus Christ, and the subject of the Bible is God's love. We can hear the voice of God's love by reading the Bible when we are worn out and discouraged, in the midst of hardship. The symbolic Bible verse is John 3:16, which is in essence the core of the Christian gospel.

For God so loved the world that he gave his one and only Son, that whoever believes in him shall not perish but have eternal life. _ John 3:16

God loved us first, while we were sinners and full of fault and mistakes, and who didn't even know God. Jesus Christ, His son paid for my sins.

We love because he first loved us. _ 1 John 4:19

This fact alone allows us to have faith of absolute positivity. We can love Him because we realized God's infinite love for us. No matter how much pain, despair, and suffering comes our way, we can look to God with faith of absolute positivity.

People who love God can live a life of absolute positivity. Fallen human beings are contaminated with sin, so they cannot find anything positive in themselves. But the cross of Jesus turned our negativity into a positivity. Therefore, we can win with faith of absolute positivity, if we trust and look to our God of love in heaven, even if we are pressed from all sides.

God chose us and called us to be his beloved children before creation. Isaiah 43:1 confirms this fact.

But now, this is what the LORD says—he who created you, Jacob, he who formed you, Israel: "Do not fear, for I have redeemed you; I have summoned you by name; you are mine." _Isaiah 43:1

Rev. Yong-gi Cho emphasized the Fourth Dimension Spirituality during his ministry, God's thoughts, God's faith, God's dream, and God's words. I think at the core of fourth dimension spirituality is the absolute positivity of God's love. If you realize the love of absolute positivity and are filled with the Holy Spirit, equipped with God's thoughts, faith, dreams, and words, you'll be able to manage God's mission.

I had seen an article previously in the newspaper, *Beautiful Companion*, about Daniel Kim who had 17 types of disabilities. The child suffered from Crouzon's disease which included ocular protrusions, breathing problems, and cerebral hypertension. He was suffering from 17 types of diseases. Doctors said there was no chance of survival. Even if this child lived, he would not see, hear, or walk. In fact, he ate with a hose through his nose until he was six years old, and he walked for the first time when he was eight. To say a word, he had to press the tube inserted in his neck with a finger and speak. And yet he always said he's happy. I confess that I'm thankful. The child has now become a teenager after dozens of surgeries. He not only sees, hears, and talks, but also walks and runs. He even conveys his ambition to become a hospital chaplain and help and comfort people who are suffering from diseases like him. Even if we had one disability or problem, resentment and complaints would probably follow, but this child made this confession with 17 disabilities. "I am happy. I am thankful. It is because God loves me."

God who shines light amidst the darkness

Among the children's favorite art activities, is one called the mosaic. You can create a mosaic by tearing off colored paper or making patterns to create a mosaic. Both bright and dark colored paper are needed to create a mosaic. You can't create a nice picture with bright colors alone. A beautiful work of art is created only when bright and dark colors are used and arranged well. The same goes for our lives. The things that brought us difficulty, the people who made us cry, and the painful memories that hurt us can combine to create a wonderful picture of life.

There are people who ask this question. If God is alive, if God is the God of love, why is there so much suffering and evil in this land? But surely, we can find God's truth and love even in hardship. You can experience God's goodness and His ability to turn evil into good. You realize that God's hand is behind everything between good and evil.

I form the light and create darkness, I bring prosperity and create disaster; I, the LORD, do all these things. _ Isaiah 45:7

Both light and darkness is created in God's hand. God has created peace; God has also created hardship. Therefore, whether it's in brightness, darkness, peace, or trouble, we must leave everything to God. In all things, God works together for the good in the lives of such people.

God makes history behind good things and makes good history even behind evil things. Moses survived when the Pharaoh of Egypt killed all the boys. He became the princess's adopted son and accomplished God's work. The crucifixion of Jesus, who was sinless, could also be seen as the most evil thing in history. The Jews and the Roman governor, Pilate, put their strength and motive together to kill God's son on the cross, they created the worst situation. However, this became the best event in God's providence. As a result, all mankind is saved by faith through Jesus and is blessed with eternal life. Even if the devil makes the worst, God can make it the best.

Words also change depending on how you make up your mind. Your facial expressions and behaviors change. Your values and beliefs change. In the end, life changes depending on your mind. Having faith in Jesus in our heart means being a person of absolute positivity. For a believer, failure is not failure, and despair is not despair. For Joseph, the 13 years of hardship were not failures, but rather the way to God's blessing that was prepared. It became the way to save himself and save the people. Hardship is a blessing, a blessing in disguise.

Joseph, a dreamer, had to go through a lot of trouble because of his dream. He was betrayed by his brothers and sold as a slave, and he was unfairly imprisoned. But Joseph prayed in all his adversity solely trusting in God. In the end, the hardships worked together for good, and he became the prime minister of Egypt. Later, when his father died and his brothers were afraid of Joseph's revenge, Joseph made this confession.

You intended to harm me, but God intended it for good to accomplish what is now being done, the saving of many lives. _ *Genesis 50:20*

He said that although his brothers treated him badly, God turned it into a good outcome. Joseph confessed with the faith of absolute positivity that everything is God's providence. Therefore, don't resent or complain when you are in trouble, but trust and pray for God's sovereign love and providence.

Job, a righteous man in the East, suffered from loss of property, loss of family, and loss of health. His wife also shared in his hardship. She said, "Curse God and die." But in all these circumstances, he did not sin nor did he resent GodJob 1:22. How could God not be happy with Job? Job's belief in positivity eventually became a source of overcoming all difficulties and being blessed twice as muchJob 42:10.

No matter how difficult and hard life is, if you have faith of absolute positivity, you will experience the power of God who works all things together for good. God wants to bless us and give us dreams and desires.

For I know the plans I have for you, declares the LORD, "plans to prosper you and not to harm you, plans to give you hope and a future." _ *Jeremiah 29:11*

There is no loss for a life of prayer

We can pray and forget but God does not forget but responds. God gives the response in three ways: 'Yes, no, and wait.' God responds with 'yes' every time we pray pleading for His will. What should I do if I prayed sincerely to God and he doesn't seem to respond? Even in this situation, you have to wait with positive thoughts and faith because God has prepared something much better than what you think. And He gives us something better at the appointed time.

If you prayed with intent and didn't get a response at the time you wanted, God didn't fail to respond. There may be a time later which is better than now, so it may not be answered at the moment. God has a better plan, further, He has the best plan. Therefore, we should not think of unanswered prayers as God's rejection. Please remember this. "There is never a case where we are at a loss for praying to God."

When I served as president of Bethesda University in the United States, Dr. Delta, president of the Assemblies of God Theological Graduate School visited me and told me the following story. It's a story when he was serving at a seminary in Togo, West Africa. An elderly and inarticulate student who barely graduated from the seminary went to a village to plant a church. However, it wasn't easy to evangelize because the village's chief was a shaman. Eventually, the minister, packed up to go somewhere else because in the eight years, he only gained three believers. However, as he left the village, he heard God's voice when he prayed for the last time. "When did I tell you to leave?"

He repented with tears and returned to the village. The chief's son was dying of a fever, wrapped in blankets in his yard. Next to him was a note from the chief, "save my son because Jesus, the God you believe in, heals diseases. If my son dies, you will die because you have lied for eight years." He prayed earnestly with all his might and then a miracle happened. The chief's son's consciousness returned. That event led to 1,400 out of 1,800 villagers, including the chief's family, believing in Jesus.

Jesus Christ is the same, yesterday, today, and forever. Jesus still lives, and is at work, and is with us. So, look at your situation and don't give up. When you hold on to the word of God's promise and move on with faith, He will work in the best time and in the best way.

None of the prayers we offer with faith is a loss. Everything will change beautifully in God's time. After a dark night, a bright morning comes. Therefore, you must believe in God's faithful love. In a letter to the believers in the Corinthian church, the Apostle Paul said, "God is faithful."2 Corinthians 1:18 In other words, it means, "God never disappoints those who faithfully believe in Him." That's right. If we believe in the God of absolute positivity, we will always be victorious1 Corinthians 15:57.

Faith of absolute positivity that brings miracles

I went to the United States to study abroad on July 31, 1982. About three years after I started studying abroad, something unexpected happened. On the first week of February 1985, a pastor in charge of Full Gospel Church in Washington suddenly resigned, which led me to serve the church. I prayed to God how to minister. Then God ordered to build the right image of a shepherd and to build a church. However, upon arrival at the church, the church was in no condition to build.

Only three members attended the Friday night service when I took over for the first time. After contacting all the members, a total of 57 attended the following Sunday service. In addition, the church's finances at the time had a balance of $14,000, which was 12 million KRW for the exchange rate at the time. At least 3 billion KRW was needed to build the church. We couldn't even start building but I prayed with faith of absolute positivity and dreamed with the members. I cried out for the construction of the church, believing in it. And on a weekly basis, I made the members greet each other by declaring, "The church has been built."

To my surprise, God blessed and opened the way. About six years after my first dream, a beautiful church was built. We were able to buy about 2.5 acres of land and complete a church that could accommodate 1,000 people. We were able to cover construction costs and land purchases of $2.7 million without any bank loans. At first, we started empty-handed, but God worked as we believed, as we dreamed, and as we said.

At that time, there was a person who always spoke negatively and criticized the pastors and the church while I pastored there. I was so heartbroken and exhausted; I complained to God like this. "Lord, can you send him somewhere else? I'm having a hard time." And the Lord said this. "If he goes somewhere else, someone worse than him will come." At first, I didn't understand what I was saying, but after a while, I found out that the situation was a "thorn" that God gave me. I always prayed for him despite my weary heart, and then one day the Lord told me, "Bless him." When I prayed prayers of blessing, God poured out compassion for him. Through this experience, I was able to learn how to be victorious in God's tests, have mercy on others, and bless them. Thanks to the faith of absolute positivity that I learned from Rev. Yong-gi Cho, I was able to overcome my difficult times studying overseas, financially, physically, and mentally, and learned to endure a ministry that could've been more difficult than it already was.

One time I received a call from a deacon in the evening. Since the husband was in critical condition, I asked her to bring him to Fairfax Hospital as soon as possible. When I rushed to the hospital, the doctor told me that he was in an emergency due to the worsening cirrhosis of the liver and that he would die in a few hours because he had eight holes in his stomach. He was bleeding. At the doctor's word, the son-in-law was calling the funeral home. I was about to enter the intensive care unit to pray, but the deacon grabbed me and said, "While praying, God said. If the pastor comes and prays, he'll heal my husband. Please lay your hands over him and heal my husband."

The Lord didn't tell me that, but the situation was so dire that I prayed desperately. The deacon kept shouting 'amen' during the prayer. But from the time I returned home, miracles began to occur.

That night, to my surprise, the bleeding stopped, the fluids exited his stomach, and his consciousness returned. They said he wouldn't be able to make it through the night, he moved to a general hospital room the next morning and lived for more than 30 years after that.

God is the God of miracles. God does what humans can't. Healing and change occur when we move forward with the faith of absolute positivity. It's like touching the hem of the Lord's garment. Miracles will happen if we anticipate, pray, and wait.

The water met its master and blushed

What is the address of God's house? It's our hearts. The Almighty God, who creates and rules the universe, lives in our heart. But we often think as if God is not there. I don't know how many times I get discouraged, fall to despair, or give up with a negative mind. Now, we must gather courage as we think of God who is of absolute positivity, resides within.

The faith in positivity that I emphasize in this book is not self-hypnosis or self-help. It is based on faith in God who is of absolute positivity. God is the source of all positivity. Any person, any problem, any environment, can become positive when they meet God.

In the 19th century, there was a question like this on a Religious Study examination at Cambridge University in England. “Discuss the miracle where Jesus turned water into wine.” The students were eagerly writing their answers, as one student was staring out the window. The student wrote just one line on a blank paper and left. However, the student’s answer became the perfect answer key that was recorded as a legend after the founding of the Department of Theology at Cambridge University. Here’s the short line he wrote. “The water blushed when it met its owner.”

The main character who wrote the legendary answer was George Gordon Byron, one of the three great romantic poets in England. The feature poem, Pilgrimage 1812 by Child Harold, which he traveled and published in Europe, gained tremendous praise and popularity. He left this impression at the time. “One morning, I woke up and found myself famous.”

Life changes when you meet the owner of your life. In chapter 2 of the Gospel of John, we see a wedding feast in Cana run out of wine. Anyone can see that it was a short coming and blaming could’ve occurred. However, Jesus showed an amazing sign by turning water into wine. And everyone at the feast could taste the joy and the grace. When we meet God, the master of life, we can gain the best result even in the worst situation.

Our God, who is absolutely positive, is the one who creates a way where there is no way and opens closed doors. Therefore, there is no need to be discouraged or be in despair when negative environments or difficulties or hardships come our way. You only have to trust the God of absolute positivity and move forward. If you worship and trust God, you will know that everything in our lives is in God's hands.

So, you don't have to be sad or discouraged. When I look at God, who makes the bad good and the good better, I affirm myself and others. I become positive about what I do, positive about my environment, and positive about the future. I hope that all of you who are reading this book will be renewed as people with positive faith.

Positivity Quotient Check List

Positive Faith Quotient Check List?

Instructions: Please read each statement and select the most appropriate response to indicate how frequently you experience the behavior described in the statement.

Statements	Never	Rarely	Some times	Often	Always
	1	2	3	4	5
1. God is the most important person in my life and I believe I love Him the most.					
2. I believe God is with me when I pray.					
3. I believe the cross of Jesus Christ displays the love of God's absolute positivity.					
4. No matter what hardship and difficulty, I am not discouraged because God is present.					
5. I engage with God and talk to Him daily.					
6. When what I want isn't quickly achieved, I think and wait, "There will be God's timing."					
7. In my faith life, I experience and am greatly moved by God's love.					
8. When I pray, I often experience despair and negative thoughts disappearing.					
9. I read and meditate on God's Word daily.					
10. I believe that whether you're good, evil, at peace or struggling, it's all under God's sovereignty.					

After reading each statement, check the corresponding box.
Add up the checked scores for each statement.

Totals ( ) points

I praise you because
I am fearfully and wonderfully made;
your works are wonderful, I know that full well.

Psalm 139:14

Chapter 03

Fivefold Positivity(1): Positive View of Myself

The Miracle of Absolute Positivity

Chapter **03**

Fivefold Positivity(1): Positive View of Myself

> If you are positive,
> you'll see opportunities instead of obstacles.
>
> **- Widad Akrawi**

I met a lot of people while pastoring for nearly 45 years. I met many pastors and believers, people from various occupations. During the many encounters, I felt that problems of self-perception and self-positivity had a very significant impact on the maturity of life and faith.

Self-positivity determines happiness in life. It can be a starting point for failure and success. The level of self-positivity is directly related to how one draws their self-image, and it even determines the level of prayer. This also affects the growth of faith. Therefore, the first and most important factor among the Fivefold positivity is self-positivity.

The importance of positive self-image and self-esteem

A comparative life isn't a happy life. My happiness isn't defined by comparing myself to others. True happiness can be enjoyed when I live the best life that God wants. Satan's plan isn't only about obstructing God's glory, but also about making humans unhappy and miserable. So, he constantly attacks human thoughts and self-perception. He makes you have negative thoughts and low self-esteem, binding you to past hurts and anger, making you feel a sense of comparison, despair, and inferiority. Proverbs 4:23 says, from all the things you want to guard, protect your heart. "Above all else, guard your heart, for everything you do flows from it." The Word teaches us the importance of guarding our thoughts.

If you don't look at yourself through God's eyes, you can't realize your value and the meaning of life. A sense of comparison makes a person fall into a sense of poverty. In fact, those who don't respect and love themselves fall to overeating, drug use, sexual indulgence, alcohol, gambling, and game addiction. Due to the pleasures of the world, you may momentarily forget that you're miserable. However, rather than giving comfort, this behavior increases hatred for oneself and causes greater suffering. It is reported that there are more than 3 million patients who suffer from depression in Korea, and according to the survey, the first cause of depression is having an "inferior self-image."

Self-positivity is associated with 'self-efficacy'. Self-efficacy is a concept proposed by Albert Bandura, a Canadian psychologist, and refers to the expectation and belief that he or she can act appropriately in a given situation. Self-efficacy is said to be deeply related to the achievement of a given task as well as the success and happiness of life. This is because people with high self-efficacy grow into people with effort and persistence.

Dr. J. A. Hardfield, a British psychologist, told himself, "You're wrong," in his study of confidence. Statements like "I can't do anything. It's over now," and when frustrated, studies show that we can't even show 30 percent of our ability. On the contrary, statements like, "You can do it. You're a special person," adding that we are confident, shows that we can perform up to 150 percent of our actual ability.

Self-positivity is due to self-efficacy which comes from faith in absolute positivity about God. F. J. Crosby, the great American hymn writer, was six weeks old when medicine prescribed by a phony doctor was applied to her inflamed eyes. She lost eyesight due to the aftereffects. To live as a blind person for the rest of her life wasn't her choice, neither did she choose a life of suffering, this didn't happen because she made a mistake. From her point of view, it was an unfair situation where she could resent the fraudulent doctor or her parents, she could've lived an unhappy life with discouragement and despair. But F. J. Crosby met God and overcame all the obstacles and misfortunes with true faith in God. Although the eyes of the body could not see, she looked to God with eyes of the spirit and lived a life of loving and praising God.

She has written more than 9,000 hymns while living to the age of 95. She wrote hymns such as "Pass Me Not O Gentle Savior," "I am Thine O Lord, I Have Heard Thy Voice," "Take the name of Jesus with you," "Thou, My Everlasting Portion," "Blessed Assurance, Jesus is Mine," and wrote more gem like hymns, among them, is "All the Way my Savior Leads Me."Hymn 384

All the way my Savior leads me
What have I to ask beside?

Can I doubt His faithful mercies?
Who through life has been my guide?
Heavenly peace, divinest comfort
Ere by faith in Him to dwell
For I know whate'er fall me
Jesus doeth all things well

This hymn still brings great comfort, hope, and joy to countless people. God was with Mrs. Crosby. He turned her sorrow into joy and turned her pain into a song. God still pledges to care for our lives. God is with us when we move forward with faith of absolute positivity and gives us the miracle where all things go well.

I am God's masterpiece

To affirm and love yourself, you have to accept yourself as you are. The key to accepting oneself is to realize that I am a masterpiece of God the Creator. Music made by a famous composer and paintings made by a famous artist all become masterpieces. What looks like graffiti or memos to us is recognized as a work of art, precious in value. Likewise, each and every one of us is a masterpiece of God because God Almighty, the Creator made us Himself. The Bible says, "I praise you because I am fearfully and wonderfully made."Psalm 139:14 The Bible tells us that each of us is a work of art fearfully and wonderfully made.

Have you ever thought about how wonderfully the human body has been made? It takes 13,000 parts to build a car, 3 million to build a plane, and 5 million to build a space shuttle. But there are more than 100 trillion cell tissues in the human body. If you connect human blood vessels in a single line, it is said to be the length that can travel around the Earth two and a half times, more than 100,000 kilometers.

The average number of hairs for an adult is 100,000 and a strand of hair can withstand an average weight of 3 kilograms. Also, the blood of the human body is six times thicker than water, it takes 46 seconds for the blood to go around the body once, and a heart the size of a human fist beats more than 100,000 times a day. It is also said that human bones, the size of an adult's support 10 tons of weight, and the human stomach wall is completely refreshed every three days. The human skin changes once a month like changing clothes, and it is said that the skin will be renewed 1,000 times in a lifetime. It is said that the muscles of the human eye move 100,000 times a day, and when you meet someone, you like, your pupils expand to 45 percent, but when you meet someone, you don't like, your pupils shrink.

The world of creation and man are His works that show God's skill. This is why scientists say, "The human body and the earth look alike." The sun and moon resemble human eyes, rivers and water resemble blood, forests resemble hair, land resembles skin and flesh, and gold or stone resembles bones. Just as more than 70 percent of our body is water, about 70 percent of the total area of the earth, including rivers and oceans, is water. Just like the five organs and six parts of the body, the Earth is divided into the five oceans and six continents.

A person is born into this world as a baby, grows up as a young man, after the middle ages, reaches old age. This is similar to the blooming season of spring, lush green summer, bearing fruit in autumn, and thinning with white hair like the winter. "He who fashioned and made the earth, he founded it; he did not create it to be empty, but formed it to be inhabited—he says: 'I am the LORD, and there is no other.'" Isaiah 45:18

God created the shape of each one of us Psalm 139:15, and what is surprising is that the human appearance, the brain and the organs, all of them are unique. According to people who study waves, even if the waves hit hundreds of millions of times, every shape of the wave is different. Even if it snows a lot in the winter, each snowflake's shape is different. Even if there is a lot of sand on the beach, there is no sand particle that is the same. How surprising is this?

The same goes for humans. There's no one in the world who looks the same. Siblings born from the same mother's belly are all different. If you look closely, twins are different. Each person's hair is different, and the shape of their nails are different. My palm lines are different, my voice is different. How amazing is that? There isn't a single person like you in the world. There is only one person like you in the history of mankind and the universe.

Pablo Ruiz Picasso's painting is worth billions of won, and Leonardo da Vinci's "The Mona Lisa" is worth tens of billions of won. How valuable are we, the works of God? We are created by God Himself, the greatest creative artist. Therefore, you should acknowledge your beauty and self-worth, and live with self-respect.

A new self-image gained through the lens of the cross

There was a king who loved pink. So, he ordered that everything in the palace be changed to pink. The king was pleased to see that the royal family was all pink. He went further and ordered the whole country to be turned pink. The servants changed the roof of the house where the people lived to pink, the clothes to pink, and the mountains to pink at the king's command. The king was very happy to see the whole country turned pink, but it was unfortunate that the sky was still blue.

"How can I turn the blue sky into a pink sky?" The king was torn. No matter how much he thought about it, he couldn't think of a way to change the color of the sky. Eventually, he visited his teacher and asked her to tell him how to turn the sky pink. The teacher listened to the king and asked for a week. A week later, the king wondered what clever trick his teacher would give him. The teacher gave the king pink glasses and said, "If you wear these pink glasses, the sky will turn completely pink." The king was so excited with the pink glasses on because the whole world looked pink as his teacher said.

It's important to know what lens we use to see our self and our life. You can't see yourself precious and valuable with the lens of being unloved, with discouragement, feelings of inferiority, and negative thoughts. We cannot move towards the future that God wants. The lens that we have to put on is the lens of the cross of Jesus Christ. You have to look at yourself through the lens.

We can realize two important truths through the cross. First, we can see the price of our sins. Our sins were so great and so heavy that they could never be solved without God's only son. Second, you can see how much God's love is. God loved us enough to willingly give up his son. The cross shows how great the sin of man is and how great the love of God is at the same time. Therefore, I must feel the great love of God the Father through the lens of the cross and increase my self-esteem.

The Bible tells us that we are a chosen people, a royal priesthood, a holy nation, God's special possession1 Peter 2:9. It isn't because we have qualifications or merit, but we have received God's choice. God loved us while we were still sinners and called us to be childrenJohn 15:16; Ephesians 1:5. We are also able to go before the throne of God with the power from the King through the blood of Jesus. We are a holy nation that is distinguished from the world. The kingdom of heaven is in me. Just as a famous person's possession increases its value, we have great value because we belong to God Isaiah 43:1.

Seeing myself through the lens of the cross is like having a positive view of oneself. When I realize the immense grace and love of God, who has saved a sinner like me, I know my value, which is the basis for living with absolute positivity and absolute gratitude. When we do that, our thoughts and prayers change and our dreams and visions change.

Three wishes of a certain beggar

There was a kind-hearted beggar who was nice and not greedy. One day, God appeared to the beggar and said, "I will grant your wish, so tell me three things." The beggar was thinking about what to wish for, and with his first wish, he said he wanted an aluminum can. This is because if you have an aluminum can, you can put a lot of rice and side dishes when you beg. God allowed the beggar an aluminum can.

God asked, "Now what is your second wish?" Then the beggar said he wanted a stainless steel can this time. He needed a stronger material can than aluminum. God allowed that, too.

God said, "Now what is your last wish, I will grant you everything you ask." After thinking for a long time, the beggar said, "God, here's my last wish. Please allow me to have a thermos." He needed a thermos to keep his food warm by putting rice or side dishes he received from begging.

Why did this beggar wish for such things? This is because he still perceived himself as a beggar. He stood before God Almighty, but his level of prayer was only that much because he had a self-image of a beggar. A positive future begins with a positive self-image and positive thoughts.

> *Now to him who is able to do immeasurably more than all we ask or imagine, according to his power that is at work within us.*
> *_ Ephesians 3:20*

Self-images determine the level of thought and the level of prayer. Like the ten spies who came back after spying the land of Canaan and reported it negatively, "We seemed like grasshoppers in our own eyes."Numbers 13:33 If this is what you're thinking, you cannot conquer the land of Canaan. If you don't have a self-image of faith, you can't move towards the future and vision that God has planned. We must now realize our precious worth before God. I hope this will raise the level of thought and prayer.

Positive view of self and love for others

Those who are positive about themselves and love themselves can love God and others. Your attitude towards yourself is like a lens that looks at others. It's the same principle. It looks convex when viewed through a convex lens and concave when viewed through a concave lens. Likewise, a person who cannot see himself with a lens of love cannot see anyone else with a lens of love. If you consider yourself insignificant, others will feel it and treat you as insignificant.

Self-love and self-centeredness should not be confused. Self-centeredness is the result of negative self-image, not self-love. As philosopher Erich Pinchas Fromm put it, selfishness and self-love are false self-image polarities. Conversely, denying one's strengths and consciously revealing only flaws or failures leads to a psychological destruction process, not humility.

If you can't love yourself, you can't love others. Ephesians 5:28 says, "Like this, husbands will love their wives like themselves, so those who love their wives love themselves." The phrase "If you love your wife, you love yourself" implies that "He who loves himself can also love his wife." If you expand and apply it, you can see that those who love you can love their husbands, children, and those who love you can love others.

Jesus said, "Love your neighbor as yourself." James 2:8 This word implies, "You have to love your body, that is, yourself, so that you can love your neighbor as much." We must remember that self-love as well as neighborly love is included in keeping the best laws. Self-love and neighborly love are two sides of a coin. We can love God and our neighbors depending on how much we love ourselves. If you love yourself a lot, you can love your neighbor a lot, and if you love yourself less, you love your neighbor less.

John Powell said this in the book, *Through seasons of the heart.* "If you feel disappointed and empty about yourself, you lose the desire or motivation to go to your neighbors, and if you are positive and satisfied with yourself, you can reduce your pain and listen to your neighbors' needs." As such, self-love has a profound impact on interpersonal relationships.

Self-love includes a mind that values one's personality, one's trust, one's firm confidence, and one's recognition of the value of others. Proverbs 23:7 says, "For he is the kind of person who is always thinking about the cost." If we want to know what the other person is like, we need to know first what the person thinks of himself. Respect and affirm yourself first so that you can love your neighbors and create happy interpersonal relationships.

Your weakness can become your strength

Another important factor in self-positivity is the thorough recognition of one's weakness in front of God. Self-positivity is different from mere confidence or arrogance. A person who affirms his weakness can be humble. And a person with a humble attitude can rely entirely on God. Only absolute positivity of God gives us strength and courage and moves us towards a vision with confidence.

Edison was deaf, but he invented the phonograph, John Milton was blind, but is praised as Britain's greatest poet. John Bunyan wrote the Pilgrim's Progress in an icy prison. Louis Pasteur discovered the basic principle of being immune to disease without being able to use the body freely. Their common characteristic is that they did not live a life marked by discouragement because of their weaknesses. Rather, they used their weakness as an opportunity to leap in a better direction.

Abraham, Isaac, and Jacob were called the ancestors of faith, but they were people who had many faults, including lying, deceiving, making mistakes, and falling. But God chose them as people of faith, trained them, and used them. So are the cases of Moses, David, and Paul, the other figures of faith. They were even murderers, aiding and abetting murderers. The greatest sin that man can commit is murder, and how great is God who used those who committed these murders. The people of faith are not great, but the God who used them is great.

Even though I'm weak, have faults, or circumstances may be difficult, I can always renew my mission with faith of absolute positivity and a new self-image. Even if I have pain and a thorn, I know that God gives me new grace and power. We must remember that God gave Paul a thorn in his body for fear that he might be spiritually prideful. Paul, who realized the meaning of the thorn, confessed like this.

But he said to me, "My grace is sufficient for you, for my power is made perfect in weakness." Therefore I will boast all the more gladly about my weaknesses, so that Christ's power may rest on me.

That is why, for Christ's sake, I delight in weaknesses, in insults, in hardships, in persecutions, in difficulties. For when I am weak, then I am strong." _2 Corinthians 12:9-10

In God, everything can be new and all things can come together for good. If I believe that God loves me and has an amazing and good plan for my life, I will experience the miracle that any weakness can be a strength and any curse can become a blessing.

Bless yourself with self-fulfilling prophecy

Good prophecy refers to speaking and proclaiming God's thoughts and words with the heart of God's love. Prophecy is directed at the church, at others, and at the community, but it must be first applied to self. The prophet Joel prophesized that in the end times when the Holy Spirit is in fullness, regardless of age, men and women will have dreams and visions through the word of GodJoel 2:28.

God said to Abraham, "You will be a blessing." He blessed Abraham with a great nation and a great name and blessed all menGenesis 12:2. He was promised not only to be blessed, but also to be the source and channel of blessing. He said those Abraham blesses He will bless because he made him a blessing, God will curse those who curse himGenesis 12:3.

Today, the same is for us as descendants of Abraham's faith. When we believed in Jesus, we were already blessedGalatians 3:14. Not only will I be blessed, but many will be blessed through me. Therefore, I must declare with blessing to myself. Put your name in it and bless it. "Hey, you've already become source of blessing. Many will be blessed by heaven and earth through you!"

Prophecies are often associated with the future. God did not judge Abraham, Peter, or Jacob by their present appearance and their faults. God saw Abraham as the father of the nations, Peter as the stone to build the house of God, and Jacob as the holy nation of God by changing his name to Israel. The love and expectation God has in my life is much greater and greater than I think.

If I realize that God loves me, I must prophesy and bless myself with that love. Look in the mirror and declare. "You are the child of God. You are a channel for blessings. The love of God will flow through you. Your community will be changed through you. The fullness and healing power of the Holy Spirit will come unto you. You are a rich man. Many good things will happen to you." Our lives will change according to God's thoughts, faith, dreams, and words.

The miracle of absolute positivity can happen to me and to you. To experience this miracle, you must be able to have a new positive mind about yourself. From today, let's look at ourselves through the lens of the cross and draw a new self-image. You need to restore your spiritual worth and self-image of prosperity. You have to realize the mission of your life and bless yourself spiritually. In that case, God's overflowing blessing will come to us. I hope that the abundant grace of self-positivity overflows in all of you.

Positivity Quotient Check List

Positive View of Myself Quotient Check List?

Instructions: Please read each statement and select the most appropriate response to indicate how frequently you experience the behavior described in the statement.

Statements	Never	Rarely	Some times	Often	Always
	1	2	3	4	5
1. I think I'm attractive.					
2. I don't compare myself with others and feel inferior.					
3. I believe that God made me unique and precious.					
4. I think I have enough qualifications to be loved.					
5. I feel happy now.					
6. I am not swayed by people's gossip or criticism.					
7. I believe that I have talent and value.					
8. I value and love myself.					
9. I think I can do well with whatever I'm entrusted with.					
10. I picture my future self as I declare and bless my future.					

After reading each statement, check the corresponding box.
Add up the checked scores for each statement.

Totals ( ) points

Be kind and compassionate to one another,
forgiving each other,
just as in Christ God forgave you.

Ephesians 4:32

Chapter 04

Fivefold Positivity(2): Positive View of Others

The Miracle of Absolute Positivity

Chapter **04**

Fivefold Positivity(2): Positive View of Others

> Write injuries in dust, benefits in marble.
>
> **– Benjamin Franklin**

The second part of the Fivefold positivity is a positive view of others. We must continue to renew our mind and perspective, so we see not only ourselves positively in light of the cross but also see others in the same positive perspective. Pastor Dietrich Bonhoeffer of Germany, who wrote the song we often sing "Von guten Machten" once said, "He who meets God meets his brother. Those who meet God see the brother's face as God's face, but those who do not meet their brothers cannot meet God. Also, God's own brotherhood in Christ is to allow us to see him again behind all brothers." If you truly meet God and change, you can feel God's heart for others and even respect themRomans 12:10.

God's still small voice

Anne Gardell, a renowned American psychologist, was born with a cleft lip, gums, and suffered from feelings of inferiority throughout her childhood. Unlike these days when cleft lip surgery is common, surgery to treat the symptoms was not easy at the time. Anne's face was unbalanced, teeth were crooked, and had trouble with pronunciations. So, she always stayed alone, thinking that no one could love her except her family.

Then one day, Anne's school was having the Whisper Test. A test that students stood with their backs to the door and one ear covered and the teacher would say in a small voice the sentences. "The sky is blue" and "The weather is nice today" and the students would follow it.

It was Anne's turn. Then a short sentence from the teacher's mouth changed her life. "How awesome it would be to have such an adorable daughter like you?" This brought Anne back to life. It was a moment when her negative view of herself, feelings of unworthiness of being unloved from birth was completely broken. Later, Anne said, 'The short sentence must have been put in the teacher's mouth by God. It changed my whole life,' she recalled.

Anne has a positive view of herself as a "precious and loving being" that her favorite teacher wants her to be her daughter. She gave up her negative view of herself, so she experienced recovery in her wounded mind. She is now a psychologist and is working to heal other people's minds. "I wish you were my daughter." God's heart, which was conveyed through her teacher, became a seed that would give another person a new positive view of themselves.

Zacchaeus also experienced a miracle of life changing through Jesus' whisper. Although he was rich, he had to live in contempt because he was short and had a career as a tax collector. One day, the news that Jesus was passing by was told to Zacchaeus. He went to the main street to see Jesus. There were already a lot of people gathered, and people were unwilling to give up their seats for Zacchaeus who was short. He had no choice but to climb up a sycamore tree. This is because he had a greater desire to know Jesus than to be conscious of people watching him.

Jesus paid attention to him. He stopped walking down the street and called out, "Zacchaeus!" He called him "the descendant of Abraham," Zacchaeus always received fingers and was pointed to as a sinner. Jesus' whispers toward Zacchaeus changed his negative self-perception of 'sinful', 'tax-collector', and 'short and ugly' to a positive view of himself as 'the loved one' and 'the offspring of Abraham.' As the perspective of oneself changed, so did the perspective of the future and the world. Meeting Jesus, he promised not only to return everything he had taken, but to repay it fourfold. His life became completely new.

Even if I am insignificant, and often fall and make mistakes, if you hear the whisper that God loves you, you can overcome all the trials and difficulties in the world. In addition, I know that God who loves me and loves the world, so I can love my neighbors. So, Jesus said, "Love your neighbor as yourself." Knowing that Jesus, who died for me, died for my neighbor, for those who do not seem to have anything to do with me, and for my enemy, is the driving force in embracing all neighbors with love. Therefore, those who meet the God of absolute positivity can affirm themselves, and furthermore, affirm others. You can share and deliver God's loving whisper to others.

The power of one man's encouragement

When do people struggle the most? It's when they feel left out or they're afraid of being abandoned. On the contrary, when someone truly trusts and supports you, you can overcome trials and hardships.

Professor Joo-hwan Kim, author of *Resilience* said, "We found one thing in common among children who grew properly, showing fortitude despite difficult surroundings. Among the children there was at least one adult that was part of the child's life who listened, understood and accepted the child's position unconditionally. Whether that person be the spouse, mother, father, grandmother, grandfather, uncle, aunt...."

If there's at least one person who believes in us, our lives can change. There was a soldier who experienced life change through one person's trust. Compared to his peers, his promotions were always late and because of it he experienced despair and feelings of inferiority. However, his wife comforted him. She gave strength by constantly encouraging her husband by telling him not to be discouraged and that another opportunity will come someday. Encouraged by his wife's consolation, he always did his best in the given task. He fulfilled his responsibilities faithfully even in positions that others were reluctant to take. And finally, 16 years after becoming a major, he was promoted to lieutenant colonel.

His name is Dwight D. Eisenhower. Eisenhower, who was the latest in his career to be promoted, and who wandered the humble frontier, served as the Commander-in-Chief of the United States in World War II and gave victory to the U.S. and other allies. Furthermore, he became the 34th president of the United States, helping to manage the economy stably, as well as doing away with racism and achieving world peace.

Affirming, cheering, and encouraging others can be a huge strength. As the saying goes, "Compliments can even make a whale dance," if others respect me and cheer me on with expectations, results can be improved to try to meet the expectation. His wife's words of support and positivity made Eisenhower a great soldier and an excellent leader.

Who do you say these words of support to? Your one word can save another person. The Lord always supports us and gives us hopes and dreams. He wants to spread the heart of love and words of absolute positivity through us.

The power of contact

People meet the world through contact with others. In particular, children experience the world and form self-image through physical and psychological interaction with their caregivers. John Bowlby published the attachment theory explaining child-parent bond and early childhood attachment formations are the most important factors in human nature. A scholar named Harry F. Harlow conducted the following experiment based on the attachment theory. Two infant monkeys were raised in a laboratory separating them from their mothers. The two surrogate mothers would be a wire mother with milk and a cloth mother with no milk. What did the monkeys do? When they were hungry, they approached the wire monkey, but as soon they were finished eating, they went to the cloth monkey. The monkeys wanted warm contact.

Jackie Robinson is the first African American baseball player in U.S. history to play in the major leagues. He was a member of the Brooklyn Dodgers, the predecessors to the Los Angeles Dodgers from 1947 to 1956. He was inducted into the Baseball Hall of Fame in 1962. In addition, his number 42 remains a legendary number registered as a permanent member of the entire club. African American athletes are now common in all sports, regardless of the type of game, but white supremacy was prevalent in the United States when Jackie Robinson was active. As a baseball player he had to suffer discrimination and ridicule because baseball was considered a sport for white people.

One day, he made a defensive error. The crowd booed, and even the fellow players did not hide their abusive language and unpleasant expressions. At the height of the gruesome atmosphere, Harold Peter Henry Reese also known as "Pee Wee" Reese, was in the shortstop position. He approached Jackie Robinson, took off his glove and hugged him. The two laughed and talked. The atmosphere of the stadium changed in an instant. Jackie Robinson said at that time that he was reborn. Without the encouragement of Harold Peter Henry Reese, perhaps the legendary player would not have existed.

When you're having a difficult time, is there anyone you can run to and hug? God is always waiting for us and is paying attention to us with warm eyes. The psalmist confesses to God.

God is our refuge and strength, an ever-present help in trouble.
_ Psalm 46:1

When anxiety was great within me, your consolation brought me joy.
_ Psalm 94:19

When you are in God's arms, all your worries and fears disappear. People's view of us and worries about tomorrow can't make us unfold. God's love raises us back up and we become victorious with faith of absolute positivity. Furthermore, with the power of love, we can reach our neighbors and encourage them. Strengthened by God's love, we can reach out our hand in encouragement to the souls that are worn out and exhausted, sharing our experience on the power of God's love.

Gottman's 5:1 Ratio

The secret to improving the taste of food is to season it well. No matter how expensive and good the ingredients are, you can't make delicious food if you lose the balance of taste, such as salty and sweet, spicy, and bitter, and sour. So, when people make food, they try to follow famous recipes, and they also pay to get recipes from famous restaurants.

Just as recipes are important when making food, recipes are important for relationships between people. Dr. John Gottman, a world-renowned expert and authority on marital and family relationship therapy, advises that "the way we talk" is the most important factor in determining happiness. After 39 years of observing and studying 3,600 couples, it isn't the content of the fight, but rather, their approach that amplifies conflict and sickens the relationship. It has been shown that couples who maintain good relationships use more positive approaches such as being considerate and appreciative, gratitude and more positive methods, whereas couples that are divorcing use more negative methods such as criticism and contempt. So, Dr. Gottman presents specific numbers that are present in happy relationships, the ratio of positive to negative language is 5 to 1. This is known as "Gottman's 5:1 Ratio." In other words, you should use five times more positive words than negative words.

This not only applies to marital relationships but any relationship where positive consideration makes you look forward to the next meeting. You'd be reluctant to meet someone who uses cold words without hesitation or makes a face of criticism. Think of Nahor's insulting remarks and Abigail's humble attitude. Abigail's self-lowering words and hospitality for the travelers not only prevented David's crimes but also preserved the lives of her herdsmen and servants. She also gave herself a chance to be elevated1 Samuel 25.

More than 90 percent of U.S. prison inmates grew up with indifference and negative comments from their parents. People who grow up hearing negative things eventually end up living an unpleasant life in the future. However, when you grow up hearing positive words such as, "You're worth it. You can do it," a positive future opens. What about you? Do you use a lot of negative words? Do you use a lot of positive words? Please remember that positive words are important for good interpersonal relationships and happiness in life.

Wisdom of positivity that impacts conversation

When you talk to others, you need wisdom to speak in positive words. Once upon a time, an emperor in Turkiye had a dream. It was a strange dream where all of his teeth fell out. As soon as he woke up, he asked a wise man to interpret his dream. The wise man said, "Your Majesty, it's a very sinister dream. The loss of teeth means that all your loyal subjects will die one by one." Then the emperor became angry, ordering, "What? How dare you say such an ominous thing? Drag this man out of here right now and punish him by paddling him 50 times."

Another wise man was called out by the emperor. Hearing the

dream, he said. “Your Highness, that dream is a good omen. It’s a very good dream. It means that your Highness lives longer than all his other subjects.” When the emperor heard this interpretation, he was delighted and told him to take 50 gold pieces from the treasurer. At the time, the treasurer said to the wise man, “Your dream interpretation is very different from the first dream interpretation story. The servants die first, but the emperor lives longer.” Then the wise man smiled and spoke. “That’s right. A person can talk a lot, but the important thing is how you say it.”

When you talk to others, it is important to express your words wisely. There is a saying in our country that “even the same words are different depending on how you say it.” You should refrain from words of criticism and condemnation and speak words of wisdom that helps others.

This is an anecdote that Hwang Hee Jeongseung, told during the Joseon Dynasty. He retired and was on his way home when he met a farmer who was plowing rice paddies with two cows. He asked the farmer an insinuating question. “Which of those two cows work better?” And the farmer stopped what he was doing and walked up to him. Then, whispering, “Oh, yes, black cows work better than yellow cows.” When Hwang Hee Jung-seung said, “Why do you come all the way here and talk?" The farmer replied like this. "The cows are listening too. The cows don't feel good when they hear comparisons."

Don't criticize others easily. Jesus said, "Don't criticize, and you won't be criticized Do not judge, and you will not be judged."Luke 6:37 According to Revelation, when God's salvation and kingdom is fulfilled, it is said that "For the accuser of our brothers and sisters, who accuses them before our God, day and night, has been hurled down."Revelation 12:10 One of the devil's names is 'Diablosδιάβολος'. The English word devil, comes from this word 'Diablos.' It means 'the one who slanders, the one who mocks.' Satan slandered God when he overthrew Adam and Eve. He also made Adam slander Eve before God. Since then, demons have caused people to sin and making churches fall through powerful weapons of mockery and slander. So, the one who slanders much resembles the devil's character.

We must say words that are beneficial. We must speak words that are full of grace. "Don't say anything dirty but say what is good and helpful for building others up according to their needs, that it may benefit those who listen."Ephesians 4:29 You should not say anything negative.

Benjamin Franklin said, "The secret to success lies in revealing the other's strengths without gossiping." A good word that affirms and encourages others is like a very good medicine that gives joy to the heart and keeps the body healthy. "Gracious words are a honeycomb, sweet to the soul and healing to the bones."Proverbs 16:24 The herbal medicine, which was built with positive words, has no side effects but rather excellent results. Conversations that build others up bring happiness and health to one another.

Miracle that 5 minutes of kindness brings

In his book *Give and Take*, American psychologist Adam Grant says, "Giver" is more likely to succeed than the "taker" who takes more than they're given. The "matcher" gives as much as they've received. A person who brings out the person's success succeeds, as the probability of success for the people around them increases. Giving this way may not show immediate results in short-term events such as the 100-meter dash, but it is worth it in the long-term event such as the marathon race.

Dr. Grant suggests the five-minute law of kindness as one of the skills for caring about others. I'd like to share the kindness of a man named Adam Rifkin. Rifkin did not think of getting anything back.

He just listened to another person for five minutes and showed a little kindness. His good intentions were conveyed to others, and those who received his help came to give help to others. As a result, Rifkin became a successful businessman and was named the most associated person with 640 influential people in the world by *Fortune* Magazine in 2011. Rifkin through friendly connections opened a more abundant culture of success.

Kindness and consideration make very important contributions to the success of interpersonal relationships. A kind person is liked by everyone. We like kind people and want to be around them. This is because kind people are warm and soft. One of the nine fruit of the Holy Spirit is mercyGalatians 5:22-23, which is translated as 'kindness' in the NIV English Bible. Kindness is a universal language that works everywhere.

Christian Nestell Bovee wrote: A person once said, "Kindness is a language which the dumb can speak and the deaf can hear."

Abraham, the ancestor of faith, welcomed three sojourners who passed by with kindness treating them warmlyGenesis 18. Abraham treated them with butter, milk, and veal, and one of the sojourners was Jesus. Eventually, Abraham received God and His messengers, and at the age of 100, he received the word of promise and blessing for his son Isaac. When we treat people, we should treat them as if we were being treatingMatthew 10:40-42.

This is the story of a deacon in our church. In 2011, the deacon's son was diagnosed with a rare tooth disease, and there was no exact name or treatment. As time went by, the condition only got worse. Then, he attended our church at the recommendation of his mother's friend, a senior deaconess. One day, six months after praying day and night, God gave me confidence in healing. After that day, the son's condition began to improve noticeably, and in 2013 recovered completely after receiving prayer where I laid hands. The deacon met Jesus in the absolute despair of his son's disease and experienced God's grace for treating his son, so he couldn't stay still. So, he decided to live for the sick and struggling people and became a social worker and started serving the disabled, the homeless, and the youth.

Then one day, when he passed by a road that he didn't usually take because he had an appointment, he met a homeless person who was sitting alone. He could feel that he was different from any other homeless person with white and fine skin, and it turned out that he was a developmentally disabled person. Due to the nature of people with developmental disabilities, there was a lot of caution against strangers, so the deacon greeted him daily and created a relationship with him. He was able to share a meal with him in a month. And that day, the deacon heard something shocking from him, "No matter how much I pray, my mom isn't breathing, and she isn't coming back to life. My mom is still at home." The deacon hurried to visit the house with the police to help with the funeral. The deacon said, "I think God sent me, 'You should go there,' through an angel who looked homeless." God sent the deacon for this family who had a developmentally disabled son and did not know what to do after his mother's death.

God calls us to a place of serving and wants to use it as a channel of blessing. The love and blessings we have experienced we should pass onto more people. If we give love and kindness to others, it will come back to us like a boomerang.

Melt the heart of your enemy with love

The United States no doubt but also the world, Abraham Lincoln, the president of the United States is one of the most well-known figures. He is at the center of giving freedom to the African Americans, he is also in the center of the smallest American currency, the penny. There was a man named Edwin Stanton who had been bullying and gossiping about Lincoln for a long time. He said, "Everyone, we don't have to go all the way to Africa to see gorillas. If you go to Springfield, Illinois, you can see the original gorilla," he said in an insulting remark. He didn't stop saying rude things even after Lincoln became president. When Lincoln passed by, tall and long armed, he criticized his political power by saying, "There goes a monkey with long arms," and "I don't know if there's any set principles, no consistency in behavior, no intellectual understanding."

But Lincoln didn't respond at all. Even after becoming president, he did not take any legal action or punish him. Rather, he appointed him as Minister of Defense. Lincoln's staff said, "Sir, how can you put a man like him, the enemy who has tormented you so much in an important position? We need to get rid of those people." Then Lincoln replied. "I think so, too. We need to get rid of the enemy in our hearts. However, it does not mean to kill and destroy the enemy, but to melt them with love and make them a friend. Jesus also told me to love my enemy. Now he's not my enemy. "I'm glad that I have no enemies, and I'm glad that I can get help from such a capable person."

Lincoln's choice was right. Many people praised Stanton for his outstanding performance. And when Lincoln was assassinated, he was the first to run and embrace Lincoln. Weeping, he said, "Here lies the greatest man in the world." Lincoln not only called sinners righteous, but also knew and practiced God's love for calling them beloved children. Therefore, rather than trying to repay Stanton for criticizing and despising him, he gave him a chance. And he was able to make him his own person and friend.

The Bible says, "Be kind and compassionate to one another, forgiving each other, just as in Christ God forgave you."Ephesians 4:32 Anyone who believes that God loved us first, we who are full of sin and faults, Jesus who hung on the cross for us, we can forgive and love others. We are the ones who had been forgiven of 10,000 talents in debt. Knowing that our debt has been cleared, the debt so great that we couldn't even repay it even if we were to pay our whole life, then we can have a heart of forgiveness for the one who owes 100 denarii. We can forgive the one who hates and resents us, is envious and jealous of us.

God called and met us who were groaning in absolute despair. The God of absolute positivity has allowed us to live a life of absolute hope now. We can never enjoy this grace alone, knowing how we have been transferred from darkness to light, from death to life. We can't help but introduce the God of positivity to those around us. Now we must encourage, build people up, treat them kindly, forgive, and love them with God's love. Those who know of their value can affirm the precious value of others and live a positive life.

Positivity Quotient Check List

Positive View of Others Quotient Check List?

Instructions: Please read each statement and select the most appropriate response to indicate how frequently you experience the behavior described in the statement.

Statements	Never	Rarely	Some times	Often	Always
	1	2	3	4	5
1. When I see others, I try to see their strengths than their weaknesses.					
2. It isn't difficult to talk with someone who thinks differently than me.					
3. I'm happy to help someone in a difficult situation.					
4. I consider other people's feelings and value them.					
5. When treating others, I don't lose my smile and friendliness.					
6. I cherish the people I meet and bless them.					
7. If it's for someone else, I can take a loss.					
8. I can be friendly to people who misunderstand and hate me.					
9. I tend to encourage and praise people.					
10. I can forgive the person who hurt me or gave me a difficult time.					

After reading each statement, check the corresponding box.
Add up the checked scores for each statement.

Totals (   ) points

The Miracle of Absolute Positivity

Whatever you do, work at it with all your heart,
as working for the Lord, not for human masters.

Colossians 3:23

Chapter 05

Fivefold Positivity(3): Positive View of Work and Calling

Chapter **05**

Fivefold Positivity(3): Positive View of Work and Calling

> There are only two ways to live your life.
> One is as though nothing is a miracle.
> The other is as though everything is a miracle.
>
> **- Albert Einstein**

Reverend Cho, my spiritual mentor, always told me, "Do ministry with a joyful heart." As time passed, I realized the deep meaning of his advice. The pastor conveyed the meaning of having a clear sense of duty in his ministry and enjoying it.

Everyone in the world lives by working. Through this, we should discover God's calling and be confident in it. Therefore, it is also very important to have a positive attitude towards work. God does not work through the negative. He accomplishes great things and fulfills his mission through a person with an attitude of absolute positivity.

Blindness isn't a disability but a tool for your calling

"Pastor Younghoon Lee, how have you been? I'm Young-woo Kang. I'm in Korea now." Although he's in heaven now, Dr. Young-woo Kang often called me whenever he came to Korea. I can still recall his voice vividly. He lost his father at the age of 13 and lost his sight at the age of 14. Shocked by the news that her son was unable to see, her mother passed away shortly after, and even her eldest sister passed away due to overworking. The remaining three siblings were scattered and there was no hope before them. However, Young-woo Kang, a boy who firmly believed in God even in desperate situations, overcame all difficulties through absolute hope given by God. Young-woo Kang said, "Blindness is not a disability. It is a tool used in God's mission," he confessed.

After graduating from Yonsei University and receiving a Ph.D. in education from the University of Pittsburgh, he was appointed Chairman of the State Department's National Disability Committee in 2001 to oversee the policy of the disabled in the United States.

Even when he was diagnosed with terminal cancer, he sent a letter of thanks to his acquaintances, saying, "Thank God for giving me time to clean up at the end." Dr. Kang has always lived a life of absolute positivity and absolute gratitude. He looked at the world with positive eyes, not with negative eyes, and worked with a sense of mission in everything he did.

It is said that there are four important encounters for a person. It is expressed as 4M. It is Master, God is the Master of my life, Mate, my partner in life, Mentor, a true teacher, and Mission, a mission in life. Meeting God is the basis for completing the 4M. This is because when we meet the God of absolute positivity, we discover our mission in life.

Moses had a mission to lead Israel in the exodus, Nehemiah had a mission to rebuild the wall of Jerusalem that had been torn down. John the Baptist had a mission to prepare for the Messiah's coming by calling for people to repent, and Apostle Paul had a mission to reach the gentiles through world mission. Jesus also said, "I have come that they may have life, and have it to the full."John 10:10 So he endured the suffering and death of the cross and fulfilled his mission to save mankind.

There's no one in the world who doesn't have problems or pain. However, a person who clearly has a sense of duty in his or her life can handle any difficulty and hardship. This is because we know the pain or wounds for mission can be sublimated into stars in heaven, and tears for God can be diamonds in heaven. Above all, we must never forget the mission of worshiping and worshiping God no matter what mission we are called for and what life we live.

In God all work is holy

There are people who think that the world's work and God's work are separate. For example, pastors work for God, and church members work for the world. Some say that prayer and serving is holy, but studying and working is not.

But according to the Reformer Martin Luther, all jobs Beruf are a calling Berufung, from God. Luther says, "If a maidservant is cleaning the feces in the stable at her master's command and adheres to the duty that is a direct way to heaven. On the contrary, those who go to the church without knowing what their duties are or what they are to do, may be on their way to hell, not heaven."

God is a God who worksJohn 5:17, who rules the world through us.

Therefore, for Christians, the purpose of work and occupation is not limited to sustaining a living and realizing oneself. Through what we do, we must go as far as serving God and loving our neighbors. In that sense, the ultimate purpose of our work should be to love God and love our neighbors, not to have a reputation, status, or income in the world.

A. W. Tozer said, "If you stick to the world's profession with a holy heart, it is no longer worldly, but part of life dedicated to God." God gave us different talents and work, and among them, he made us love God and love our neighbors. Therefore, we must do our best in the position entrusted by God. Whether you're a student, an office worker, a medical worker, a pastor, a housewife, music, or a politician, this applies to everyone. Everyone has to be kind to everyone, and of course, be faithful to everything.

You must have a sense of dignity for your work

Psychologists say that when you do something, the best mind to increase productivity and efficiency is 'confidence.' Dignity in one's job means a calling and confidence in a job. Even if it's the same job, how I think about it changes my mindset about my job.

William Shakespeare, a famous British playwright, was having lunch at a restaurant, and many people greeted him politely. However, a cleaner who was watching the scene threw out a broom and sighed. This is because he felt pathetic compared to Shakespeare, who was respected and loved by many people. He saw himself sweeping the yard to earn a meal. When Shakespeare asked the cleaner why, he talked about his lamentable inner thoughts. Then Shakespeare said. "Don't lament, young man. What I do is, I beautifully describe a part of the universe with a pen, but you are responsible for beautifully managing a part of the universe that God has built with that broom. If you don't fulfill this mission, the corner of the earth that God has built will be dirty." The cleaner regained his confidence and cleaned vigorously again when his job was recognized as a vocation.

If we have the spiritual confidence of being a child of God, the king of all kings, we can do any work giving value in whatever we do with confidence. Even if it is repeated every day, you can pray to God and find meaning in it.

Repeating the same movements several times during physical training creates agility and flexibility. If you are an athlete, you have to move quickly and be flexible to get good results with muscle elasticity. Training to repeat the same motion multiple times is tedious and requires a lot of time and physical strength, but the results of these repetitive exercises are essential because they are very beneficial.

The same goes for what we do. When we work in a company or a workplace, we can do the same thing over and over again. You shouldn't complain about the small thing at this time. You have to work with a sense of duty and a positive and pleasant mind. Only then can you train your spiritual muscles and increase the reward and achievement of your work.

In a letter to the believers in the Church of Colossae, the Apostle Paul said, "Whatever you do, work at it with all your heart, as working for the Lord, not for human masters."Colossians 3:23 At that time, there were a number of slaves and servants among the Christians of the early church who worked with the gentiles. He advised these people to do whatever they do with the heart of serving the Lord. When you work with such a spiritual mission and sense of duty, you should remember that God gives the reward.

Let your magma of passion erupt

Whatever you do, you have to be passionate. Jack Welch, former chairman of General ElectricGE, was born to the son of a railway station employee and majored in chemistry at university. After graduating, he joined GE and would become the youngest president in GE history at the age of 45. During his 20-year tenure as chairman, he left behind a legend. GE's stock price rose 40 times during his tenure, and the various management innovations he led were said to have rewritten the 20th century's business administration. When he left office, a reporter asked, "If you could choose only one of the great virtues of a leader, what would you suggest?" Chairman Jack Welch did not hesitate to answer the question. "Passion!"

Jesus himself showed an example of passion, "My Father is always at his work to this very day, and I too am working."John 5:17 "As long as it is day, we must do the works of him who sent me."John 9:4 The Lord prayed devotedly in dawn prayer, night prayer, and fasting prayer, and he also worked passionately in healing, discipling, and evangelizing. Jesus was always filled with the Holy Spirit and came to bring the fire of the Holy Spirit on the earthLuke 12:49. He served, ministering even as He was on His way up to Jerusalem to carry the cross, and he also ministered by praying and forgiving while He was on the cross.

Passion is the DNA of a successful person. The writer of Ecclesiastes also said, “Whatever your hand finds to do, do it with all your might, for in the realm of the dead, where you are going, there is neither working nor planning nor knowledge nor wisdom.”Ecclesiastes 9:10

The Apostle Paul is also the epitome of a passionate minister. He was about ten years older than Jesus. In the “Acts of Paul and Thecla,” there is a description of Paul's appearance. Paul was short and bald, his legs were long, and his eyebrows were a unibrow, he also had an aquiline nose. However, his appearance was noble, and his face was full of grace. Paul loved Jesus and his passion for evangelizing the gentiles was fervent. He was 41 years old when he was first commissioned as a missionary from the Church of Antioch and 62 years old when he was martyred. So, Paul has fulfilled God's mission with a passion for missionary work for about 21 years. Because of the fire of the Holy Spirit that was moving, wherever Paul went, he lit the spirit of the cold-hearted people with the fire of the Holy Spirit.

John Wesley of England, founder of the Methodist Church, also shouted, "Light God's fire to your soul!" when England was in crisis. Our spirits must be on fire. That way, we can be passionate about what we do. The same goes for the church. The Holy Spirit fire should be lit. This way, you can live a life of faith without living a lukewarm life. We can handle the passionate duty of evangelism and mission.

Missionaries must have enthusiasm. You can't accomplish what you want doing nothing. A dependent mind that wants others to do something is not an appropriate attitude as a missionary. Enthusiasm isn't created only when there is a path. When there is passion, a way opens. The English word enthusiasm is said to contain 'in God.' We must receive energy of enthusiasm from God every day. Let's try praying this way. "God, pour Your enthusiasm into me!"

The importance of daily faithfulness

A person who is positive about work and mission is sincere. The present is a present of God's grace. It is important to live sincerely and appreciate the present every day. One of the most famous paintings by Mile Jean-Francais Millet, "The Gleaning," was originally written by Angelus. The word means "prayer offered three times a day when the bell rings in the morning, noon, and afternoon."

If you look at the painting, you see a farmer stopping at the sound of a church bell and praying reverently, and if you look closely at this painting, you realize something very important. The fact that it's not the head of a farmer or the bell tower of a church where the sun shines. The sun's rays are focused on the farming tools. It contains the profound philosophy of the painter Millet. Millet wanted to express the sacredness of labor through this painting. That's why sun rays on shining brightly on the agricultural equipment.

Labor is holy. The happiest person in the world is someone who works with a content heart. The Apostle Paul strongly recommended the church members of Thessalonica. "Make it your ambition to lead a quiet life: You should mind your own business and work with your hands, just as we told you."1 Thessalonians 4:11 We must sweat day after day and be faithful. Heaven's grace and power will not be given if we do not live earnestly. The Bible says that the lazy should learn from the diligence of ants.

> *Go to the ant, you sluggard; consider its ways and be wise! It has no commander, no overseer or ruler, yet it stores its provisions in summer and gathers its food at harvest. _ Proverbs 6:6-8*

The most important time in the world is now, and we must use the Lord's faithfulness as our foodPsalm 37:3. Just as the Lord is faithful; we too must be faithful. There is nothing free in the world and we reap what we sow in life.

Joseph Kipling, a British poet, said, "It's nothing to be loyal to the country, but to do your best to the little things in front of you by holding the tools you see." There's a saying, "Dirty is out of the place." It looks beautiful when fish swim in the river. But if the fish is lying on our bed, it can feel dirty. It's because the beautiful fish isn't in an appropriate place. Soil is essential in the fields, but if it is on the floor of the room, it's dirty and needs to be to clean. Each person has a place in life, such as a home, a workplace, and a church. When we work earnestly and faithfully in our position, we become beautiful and valuable beings.

Joseph, who was sold as a slave to Captain Potiphar due to his brothers' deceit and betrayal, was later imprisoned, being framed by Potiphar's wife. But Joseph had a consistent attitude of life in whatever circumstances he was in, and that was through 'serving.' "Joseph found favor in his eyes and became his attendant."Genesis 39:4 "The captain of the guard assigned them to Joseph, and he attended them."Genesis 40:4 The word 'serving' is repeated here. Joseph lived a life of service anytime, anywhere. In Hebrew, the word 'service עָבַד, abad' is a word used together to describe "honesty in one's work" and "a life worshiping God." Joseph faithfully worshiped God regardless of any problem or environment and faithfully handled the work entrusted to him. Daily candor becomes a mirror of a person's faithfulness.

The calling is for a life-time

We live as missionaries until we die without exceptions. Remember this and don't give up your mission or become lazy just because you're old. There are many biblical figures who have been used in their old age. Abraham was called at the age of 75, visited Canaan at the age of 90, and had a son, Isaac at the age of 100. Moses was called to exodus at the age of 80 and led the Israelites to Canaan. Caleb captured the Hebron Mountains at the age of 85. Caleb was 85 years old, but he was physically strong and mentally young. That's because he waited with anticipation for the word of God's promise. After spying the land of Canaan at the age of 40, he looked at the promise of God for 45 years.

Now then, just as the LORD promised, he has kept me alive for forty-five years since the time he said this to Moses, while Israel moved about in the wilderness. So here I am today, eighty-five years old! I am still as strong today as the day Moses sent me out; I'm just as vigorous to go out to battle now as I was then. _ Joshua 14:10-11

Caleb was strong in body and spirit because he looked towards God's dream. With the permission of his leader Joshua, he attacked and captured the mountainous region of Hebron. A person may be young but, he who does not have God's mission and dream is mentally old and spiritually weak. However, even when you get older, those who live with the word of God's promise and mission can stay mentally healthy, without getting weary, and achieve spiritual growth.

Jesus' disciples died early, but John the Apostle lived over 90 years old and was exiled to Patmos Island in the Aegean Sea. When Christianity was persecuted by the Roman Emperor, the resurrected Lord appeared to John and gave him his last mission.

On the Lord's Day I was in the Spirit, and I heard behind me a loud voice like a trumpet, which said: "Write on a scroll what you see and send it to the seven churches: to Ephesus, Smyrna, Pergamum, Thyatira, Sardis, Philadelphia and Laodicea." _ Revelation 1: 10-11

The Lord kept John alive for his mission to record the Book of Revelation, God's revelation about the end. He who has God's mission to complete cannot die. We were sent to this world on a mission. Don't make excuses about your surrounding or age and do your best until your mission is fulfilled.

George Whitfield, who started the first Great Awakening Movement in the 18th century in America, was a capable and passionate preacher who brought countless people to repentance. There were times when he preached until 1 a.m. because of his mission and passion for ministry. When his disciples said, "Pastor, you are so busy in your ministry, now take a rest," He replied, "I want to be worn away rather than rusted away." He was a revivalist who devoted himself to God's mission until his death. In this way, we will also have to maintain spiritual vitality without spiritually rusting until the Lord calls us.

Rev. Ik-du Kim of Korea passionately spread the gospel and had a healing ministry until the day he went to heaven. As a child, he was poor and had no family background, so he couldn't dream of maintaining his education. He started his business at the age of 17, but was discouraged by repeated failures, so he tried to overcome the bitterness with alcohol. Even the famous fighter in the neighborhood wasn't strong enough because Ik-du knocked him down with one punch. Time had passed by. W. L. Swallen, a missionary, was leading a rally at the time. Ik-du attended the rally and accepted Jesus at the age of twenty-seven. He was baptized by the missionary and started sharing the gospel. In Hwanghae-do province, he was rumored to pack a punch, but after believing in Jesus and sharing the gospel, he was ridiculed, stoned, and bled. Even in the midst of it all, the pastor did not give up the mission of sharing the gospel.

Since entering Pyongyang Theological Seminary in 1906, he served only one church for the rest of his life until his death in the pulpit of Sincheon Church. After a church revival meeting in October 1919, he discussed with his fellow pastors about Mark 16:17-18, "And these signs will accompany those who believe: In my name they will drive out demons; they will speak in new tongues." He prayed earnestly to God to allow him to have these spiritual powers.

Then one day, a church member whose lower jaw fell out of place 10 years prior, all sorts of methods could not fix the issue. Rev. Ik-du Kim suddenly had a great heart of love rising like a flame. Rev. Ik-du Kim fasted for three days and prayed for the member, "Please attach the fallen jaw because I believe in it," and surprisingly, a miracle occurred in which the jaw was put back together. Since that point forward, as many as 10,000 patients, including those with bent backs, Hansen's disease, lung disease, and hematopoietic disease, have been cured in the name of Jesus at Rev. Ik-du Kim's revival meetings.

At dawn on October 14, 1950, the year of the Korean War, the pastor was worshiping during the early morning prayer service at Shincheon Church, that's when the Communist Party stormed in. They fired indiscriminately at the pastor who was praying, he died on the spot. Rev. Ik-du served passionately with a sense of mission and evangelism until the day he went to heaven. We should also follow the older brothers and sisters of faith and be faithful to the work entrusted to us with a sense of duty until the day we stand before God.

Remember that God gave each person work and a mission, and work with a positivity of self-perception and a positive attitude. You must work with passion every day and live with meaning and have fun. God will surely reward to those who are faithful with the work entrusted them.

Look, I am coming soon! My reward is with me, and I will give to each person according to what they have done. I am the Alpha and the Omega, the First and the Last, the Beginning and the End.
_ Revelation 22:12-13

I hope all of you can live a happy and successful life by dedicating yourself to God's mission.

Positivity Quotient Check List

Positive View of Work and Calling Quotient Check List?

Instructions: Please read each statement and select the most appropriate response to indicate how frequently you experience the behavior described in the statement.

Statements	Never	Rarely	Some times	Often	Always
	1	2	3	4	5
1. I am enjoying what I'm doing.					
2. I think the work I'm doing is God's mission.					
3. When faced with a difficulty, rather than giving up, I rise to the challenge.					
4. I often think of ideas while I'm working.					
5. I pray to God before I go to work and pray while I work.					
6. When I work, I am kind and considerate of the people around me.					
7. I work with passion.					
8. I do my best in everything I'm entrusted with.					
9. I don't think there is work or my mission has ended because I have aged.					
10. To get better at work, I manage my physical strength.					

After reading each statement, check the corresponding box.
Add up the checked scores for each statement.

Totals ( ) points

The Miracle of Absolute Positivity

Only do not rebel against the LORD.
And do not be afraid of the people of the land,
because we will devour them.
Their protection is gone, but the LORD is with us.
Do not be afraid of them.

Numbers 14:9

Chapter 06

Fivefold Positivity(4): Positive View of Environment

Chapter **06**

Fivefold Positivity(4): Positive View of Environment

> Hope sees the invisible,
> feels the intangible, and achieves the impossible.
>
> **– Helen Keller**

Our thoughts and actions are influenced by the environment. On the contrary, the attitude we have affects the environment. The environment of various difficulties and hardships faced in life is also given to those who believe in God. But just as stars shine in the dark, the environment of hardship can be the soil where positivity could shine. The important thing here is to have a positive attitude in the face of the problem. A positive attitude is the key to breaking through the problem.

We also interact with the environment in our own communities. Therefore, it is very important to have a positive attitude towards myself, my neighbors, and the community including my church, school, company, etc.

Hurdle the wave of problems

This is the story of a couple I met at the First Full Gospel Church in Washington, USA. The couple tried everything they could to have a child, but they weren't able to for more than 20 years. They prayed hard, went to the hospital for various tests, and took good medicine and food that helped for pregnancy, but it was no use. The doctor said, "The couple couldn't have a child because the husband had a problem," the couple eventually gave up on having a child.

However, the couple heard I was in Korea. When they found out that I prayed and had a daughter after 17 years of marriage, the couple had a new dream. He said it was not possible medically, but he had faith of absolute positivity that he could have children if God helped him. As a result, the couple, had hopes again, prayed again with faith, and had a child because God gave them a miracle. At that time, the deacon was 52 years old. He received a precious child after 23 years of marriage. God gave him grace when he relied on God with positive expectations without being discouraged when there was a problem.

What is more important than the problem is the attitude towards the problem. When problems arise, we often blame others or the environment. However, this attitude does not help solve the problem at all. We should think of God's providence through problems and move forward with a positive attitude. When the ten spies who returned from spying the land of Canaan made a negative report, all of the people of Israel were discouraged. But at this point Joshua and Caleb make a confession of faith. "Only do not rebel against the LORD. And do not be afraid of the people of the land, because we will devour them. Their protection is gone, but the LORD is with us. Do not be afraid of them." Numbers 14:9 Joshua and Caleb saw the problem through eyes of faith.

One of my favorite praise song is 'Still.'

Hide me now, Under Your wings,
Cover me, Within Your mighty hand
When the oceans rise and thunders roar,
I will soar with You above the storm
Father, You are King over the flood,

I will be still, know You are God

Like the lyrics of the praise, oceans rise in our lives. The waves of problems such as family, workplace, and health problems are constantly rushing towards us. Sometimes it comes in small waves, but sometimes it comes in big waves as if it's going to sweep us away. However, he who is with the Lord is not afraid of the waves but climbs high into the sky.

A person who is afraid of waves cannot know the beauty of surfing. You can't experience the thrilling moment of flying high above the current. What waves have washed up in your life? Don't be afraid when the waves come. On the contrary, fly with the Lord above the waves. Never think negatively about any problem but break through with positive thoughts.

God, the director of my life

In July 2000, a driver crashed into a car while driving drunk. A student who was on her way home in her brother's car after studying in the library was also one of the victims of the accident. The student, who suffered third-degree burns over 55% of her whole body, was diagnosed with a first-degree facial and physical disability at the time. The student was 23-year-old Ji-sun Lee.

Twenty-three years later, Ji-sun Lee became a professor at Ewha Womans University, she returned to school, her alma mater. She says in her book, *Pretty Good Happy Ending*, "Am I the one who had an accident. Or did I meet the accident but now broken up? It took a long time to break up with the accident, and the process was slow, and my heart hurt as much as my body hurt, but eventually I broke up little by little. I didn't live as a victim of a drunk drivingDUI accident, and I didn't leave my heart there and today and every day I live in the present. … I've broken up with the accident well."

She lost all of her previous life in the car accident. All that was waiting for her were dozens of surgeries and a lot of pain. However, instead of resenting and being angry, Ji-sun Lee has looked at her situation positively creating her life day by day. She has now become a sociology professor, helping those in need and helping to foster younger students.

She says, "As life changed completely after the accident, there was an entire change in my view of God. I realized that I was a cast member in a movie that God planned, and God wrote and directed the scenario. 'I realized that I have to do my best in every scene so that this movie with a pretty good happy ending formed in God's will can be made well until the very end.' 'I was invited in God's plan,' and that made me feel more liberating."

God is the movie director of our lives. He has a great scenario for you. He has the ability to make a wonderful and heart touching movie. The joy, sadness, and every moment of life are combined to make it the best symphony. So don't panic or be afraid when you encounter a problem. Keep moving forward with faith of absolute positivity. Good things will surely happen to you.

My negative past is no longer an obstacle that entangles me

There is one thing that I realized while working in ministry. It's the fact that people who can't get out of a problem or cause problems have a common characteristic. It means that he or she is constantly reflecting on his or her mistakes and failures, as well as the wounds of their heart that they have received from others. If you are tied to the negative things you have experienced in the past, you cannot be faithful to the present and prepare for the future well.

God tells us, "Forget the former things; do not dwell on the past."Isaiah 43:18 He tells us before we do new things, like the people of Israel who took part in the exodus, we should not settle for the grace of the past but admire the new grace He has given. At the same time, it suggests that we should shake off the pains and wounds of the past. A failure in the past should be a mirror of the future and a successful past should be a steppingstone to the future. This is possible through God's power. When we come before God, He can clear our sinful past, our past failures and hurt with Jesus' blood.

Abraham had a history of deceiving his wife twice as a sister, Jacob had a history of depriving his brother the rights of being the eldest son with a bowl of bean porridge, and Moses had a history of murdering an Egyptian. Peter also had a past in which he cursed and denied knowing the Lord, and Paul had a past in which he took the lead as a witness in killing Stephen, who was full of the Holy Spirit. But their lives didn't stop there. It has been changed and used surprisingly for God's mission. Now it's time to get rid of our mistakes, wounds, and pain from our mind. Wash and forget it with the blood of Jesus.

Scholars say that forgetting is one of the important mechanisms for mental health. You have to be able to erase something that you remember to some extent so that you can come up with new ideas.

It is said that millions of trees can grow every year because squirrels forget where they hid their fruit. We must erase all the previous faults and wounds and expect a new grace and miracle from the Lord.

The book *L'Homme Qui Voulait Etre Heureux*, written by Laurent Gounelle, is famous as his nickname suggests, Happiness Evangelist. "Most of the fears we feel are creations we have created in our heads. You just don't realize it. Look at the baby learning to walk. Do you believe that the baby will succeed at once? They stand up again, and then they fall with a thud. A baby needs to fall an average of 2,000 times to learn how to walk." A child does not remember that he fell. They practice walking and happily run no matter how many times they fall. Now, we must stop reflecting on past mistakes or looking to our past wounds from this moment.

Steve Jobs had been kicked out of his company of 10 years at the age of 30, Walt Disney was fired by a newspaper company for a lack of imagination, Elvis Aaron Presley was a truck driver. Oprah Gail Winfrey was a PD who was fired by her broadcasting company because she was weak logically, Joanne Rowling was divorced and was receiving government assistance, barely making a living when she wrote a novel about Harry Potter. What these people have in common is that they have risen again through failure. All of them didn't think of failure as failure. They learned a lesson from the experience of failure and opened a new future.

According to researchers who studied Lincoln, the 16th president of the United States, shared that Lincoln suffered 27 failures in his lifetime. After overcoming 27 failures and setbacks, he became the 16th president of the United States and made remarkable history by freeing the slaves. The Wright brothers were also able to make flight after failing 805 times. Thomas Edison, who invented the light bulb, finally invented it after failing 2,399 experiments. In order to overcome problems and succeed, we need to clean our minds of our past failures and wounds in order to have a new mind and a new vision.

Remember your spiritual landmark

When I go to my childhood neighborhood, I often think of old memories. That's how powerful memories are. It is important to remember the positive experiences of the past when we encounter difficulties. David said the following fighting against Goliath, the Philistine general.

But David said to Saul, "Your servant has been keeping his father's sheep. When a lion or a bear came and carried off a sheep from the flock, I went after it, struck it and rescued the sheep from its mouth. When it turned on me, I seized it by its hair, struck it and killed it. Your servant has killed both the lion and the bear; this uncircumcised Philistine will be like one of them, because he has defied the armies of the living God. _ 1 Samuel 17:34-36

When Goliath, the Philistine general, appeared before the army of Israel, everyone trembled with fear. No one readily stepped forward in front of Goliath, who insulted God and despised Israel but David was different. He remembered God who protected him in the field. Believing that LORD, who protected him from the jaws of the lion and the claws of the bear, he boldly went to Goliath with five smooth stones and defeated him.

Landmarks refer to something symbolic, representing a place through buildings, symbols, sculptures, etc. The Statue of Liberty in New York, Big Ben in London, the Opera House in Sydney, and the Eiffel Tower in Paris are representing landmarks. Meanwhile, when we investigated what Korean landmarks foreigners thought of were the Seoul Tower, Gyeongbokgung Palace, and the War Memorial of Korea. Originally, landmarks were areas where explorers and travelers traveled to, a particular area was marked so they could return to the original spot.

1 Samuel 7:12 says, “Then Samuel took a stone and set it up between Mizpah and Shen. He named it Ebenezer, saying, ‘Thus far the LORD has helped us.’” This monument was erected by Samuel the Prophet between Mizpah and Shen to commemorate God’s help in Israel’s victory when Israel and the Philistines fought, which was later named. However, this stone wasn’t just a marker representing the region but it was a spiritual landmark that was to remind us of God’s grace.

In the journey of faith, landmarks are also needed. When we encounter difficulties and feel that God is not here or when God does not seem to respond no matter how much we pray, there is something we must think of. It is remembering the excitement of our first encounter with God, the answered prayers we received, the joy of being filled with the Holy Spirit. Therefore, we must repent and seek the renewing grace and guidance of God. If we become dull and don’t remember the grace God gave us, we can fall over and be vulnerable to temptation. However, we can pray for God’s grace again, our merciful God will give us a new miracle.

Experience breakthrough with positive prayer

Another key to breaking through the problem is the prayer of positivity. When I was appointed as the senior pastor of the Full Gospel Tokyo Church, the church was in great pain. The pastor in charge, who was previously sent from Yoido, turned all the property of the church into a corporation under his name and turned his back on Pastor Yong-gi Cho. He even kicked out the church members who followed Pastor Cho out of the church. The church members, who had nowhere to go, worshiped in the park and moved seven times in search of a place of worship. When I went, they were renting the entire four-story building to worship, but it was hard to dream of building a church because it was not easy to afford the expensive monthly rent.

I looked for what I could do in this situation, but there was only prayer. So, I devoted myself to early morning prayer for two and a half years after taking position. I prayed every day from waking up to dawn, expecting on God without blaming the environment or blaming others. Then God gave me a heart to build God's sanctuary in the hearts of the church members. He then began to open the doors into building a church according to God's way.

A deacon gave birth to a still born after seven months, leading to a funeral service in front of her stillborn covered in blood. The husband of the deacon was Japanese and asked me, "Where is my baby going now?" In Japan, cremation culture had already developed, but there was no Christian niche for the cremated ashes to be placed. Most had to be enshrined in ordinary charnel houses or in shrines or temples. After the funeral service, I prayed with a heavy heart, and the Holy Spirit touched my heart and during a Friday night worship service I declared. "Our church member gave birth to a stillborn child, but we don't have a niche for our church, so where must we rest the child? It's time to do something. I want each of you to donate money as you decide to do in your heart."

Nearly a hundred million KRW was donated that day. And the next week, more members were able to join in to prepare a niche for 450 people. The child who passed away without even a name entered the niche first. This would become the seed of building a church. The members wanted to build a church and prayed even more fervently. In addition, we began to search for a place to worship, we finally purchased an eight-story building along the main street in Shinjuku, Tokyo, and was able to build a sanctuary.

Whenever our hearts are discouraged and times get difficult, we must believe that God knows our environment and situation well. At that moment, you must move on the prayer of absolute positivity before God. "Call to me and I will answer you and tell you great and unsearchable things you do not know." Jeremiah 33:3 Even in the darkness, you must believe that all good gifts come down from the Father of Lights in heaven James 1:17. If you pray without falling into despair, you will surely see God's miracle.

Positivity in community and team synergy

There was a war in the animal kingdom. The lion became the commander-in-chief and the animals flocked from all directions. The gathered animals looked at each other and murmured pitifully. "A donkey is a dunce, so wouldn't it be better to go back because it would only interfere with the war?" "How can a coward like a rabbit fight?" "What can an ant do, it's so weak?" "Elephants are so big that they'll be caught by the enemy."

At this time, the Lion, the commander-in-chief, spoke loudly to everyone. "It's noisy. Everybody be quiet! The donkey has a long mouth and will use it as a trumpeter. And the rabbit will be used as a messenger because it runs fast, and the ant is small and invisible, so it will be sent as a guerrilla to the enemy's camp, and the elephant is strong, so it will work to carry war supplies."

In the eyes of the animals gathered for the war, each other's weaknesses were seen first. Due to the donkey's foolishness, because of the rabbit's caution, considering the ant's weakness, and concerning the elephant's large size, it seemed as if they were going to lose the war. However, the lion saw the strengths of each of the animals that gathered. Thanks to the donkey's voice, thanks to the rabbit's fast feet, thanks to the small size of the ant, and thanks to the powerful elephant, they thought they were able to win. Synergy is made when you have a positive attitude that focuses on each other's strengths within the community.

The English word "team" has this meaning.

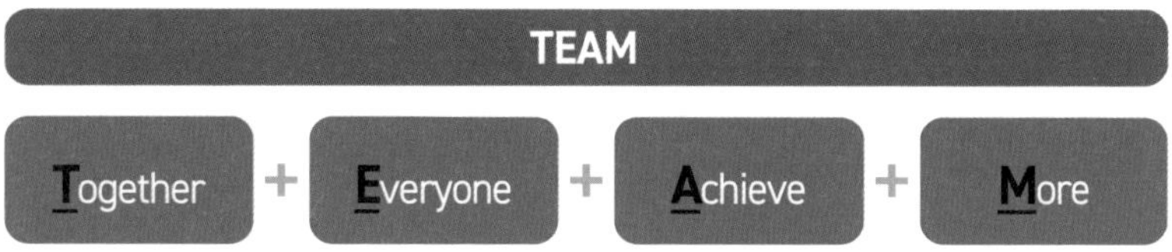

When you join forces together, wisdom that you couldn't think of alone can be exercised and greater power can be generated. This is what the Bible says, "Two are better than one, because they have a good return for their labor: If either of them falls down, one can help the other up. But pity anyone who falls and has no one to help them up. Also, if two lie down together, they will keep warm. But how can one keep warm alone? Though one may be overpowered, two can defend themselves. A cord of three strands is not quickly broken."Ecclesiastes 4:9-12

We live as part of a community, big and small. The big communities include home and school, work and church, region and country, and even the earth. We are also connected to one another. So life is not a song that you sing alone at the top of your voice, but rather a symphony that listens to each other and creates harmony. Therefore, you should look at the strength, not the weakness of the person next to you. Rather than the negative idea of 'not because of him,' you should have a positive idea of 'I will succeed in combination with his strengths.' Soon, you'll have to have a positive mind about the community you belong to.

Positive faith revives the church

Someone came to the pastor and asked him to find a church without any problems. Then the pastor responded. "There is no church without a problem. I can't tell you even if there is. The moment you enter, it will be a problematic church."

When you preach the gospel, you sometimes meet people who say, "I like Jesus, but I hate the church." There is also news that the number of so-called 'Canaan Church,' people who call themselves Christians but don't attend church, is increasing. There are people who say they want a 'no problem church.' But just as there is no life without problems, there is no church without problems. There may be a lack of church communities, and there may be churches in difficult surroundings and conditions, it is important to look at the church in a positive manner, bless and build up the church.

God called us to the body of ChristEphesians 5:30. Pastor Max Lucado explains the unity of the church in his book called *Max on Life*. The head must find reasonable answers, the eyes must see the problem, the stomach must digest the situation, the spleen must remove the bacteria, the hands must be taken cared of, and the feet must go to work."

Just as every part of the body is important, everyone in the church is important. Therefore, you must love the church you belong to, and you must love the people who belong to the church. There should be no reckless criticism or hasty judgment. Don't just look for things that stand out, but do your best, knowing that even the smallest things are precious missions entrusted to you.

In Hymnal 208, first verse, there is a lyric that goes like this. "I always love the kingdom of my Lord, the temple of the Lord, and the church that has bled." The church is the body of the Lord that the Lord has purchased with His blood. As much as the Lord loves the church, we must cherish and love the church. You should look at the church positively and fill it with an atmosphere of grace and blessing. I have to bless and pray for the church and pastor I belong to. Faith is positive. Positive faith and words saves the church.

The effects of positivity in the workplace and community

Every organization needs positive people. It is important. There was a bank president who was famous for recognizing talented people. The executive he chose to take on heavy responsibility always performed well. When people asked him the secret formula, he said, he used to call the teller on the intercom when he had to check the contract details while consulting with the customer, however, the employees' answers were largely divided into two. The first type said, "I can't go in now because I have a customer," another type said, "I have a customer, so I'll go in soon after this is over." The answers were similar in the tests, but we were able to determine whether the employee was a negative or positive person.

When hiring talent, he always made it a condition to have a positive attitude, and his choice has never been wrong.

The Metropolitan Life Insurance Company of New York, within a year had 50% of its once-expensive training recruits quit. So in order to solve this problem, they consulted psychology professors from the University of Pennsylvania. The researchers observed office workers who were good at selling insurance, and the results showed that the top 50 percent had a positive and optimistic attitude. Research showed they had 37% higher insurance sales performances and 50% lower turnover than the rest. Since then, the company has tried to recruit positive and optimistic employees when hiring new workers, which has resulted in higher sales and lower dropout rates.

If employees didn't have a positive attitude toward the company, customers wouldn't be able to have a positive attitude towards the company. Unless employees love the company, it will be difficult for customers to love the company. Furthermore, people with negative attitudes lose the opportunity to work hard or grow in an organization. Whether it's a company or employees, we need to create positive vibes.

Jane Dutton, a professor at the University of Michigan in the United States, emphasized that 'positivity' is the best weapon an individual can have. A person with positivity extends the boundless realm of possibility, which is the basis for leveraging valuable resources such as potential energy, ideas, leadership, and courage. No matter what job or community you belong to, I hope you will succeed with the 'power of positivity.'

In life, there are times when it is difficult to appreciate or affirm each other's environment. It is important to remember that a positive attitude towards the surrounding is important every time. Don't blame and resent others when you face a problem. The negative past must be cleared, reflected on God's grace, and broken through with a prayer of positivity. In addition, I have to serve and work with a positive attitude in the church or community I belong to. God will surely bless the positive people. He allows good things in our lives.

Positivity Quotient Check List

Positive View of Environment Quotient Check List?

Instructions: Please read each statement and select the most appropriate response to indicate how frequently you experience the behavior described in the statement.

Statements	Never	Rarely	Some times	Often	Always
	1	2	3	4	5
1. I don't complain when problems arise.					
2. I don't dwell on past wounds and torment myself.					
3. I believe everything that happens to me and my environment is in God's providence.					
4. I often remember the grace God gave me and gain strength.					
5. I believe God will work together for the good even in difficult situations.					
6. I tend to think positively about the community I belong to.					
7. I pray for and love the church I attend.					
8. I cherish and value my company.					
9. I don't criticize people in my community.					
10. I always have a positive attitude when I'm with or working with people.					

After reading each statement, check the corresponding box.
Add up the checked scores for each statement.

Totals (   ) points

The Miracle of Absolute Positivity

For it is God who works in you
to will and to act in order to
fulfill his good purpose.

Philippians 2:13

Chapter 07

Fivefold Positivity(5): Positive View of Future

The Miracle of Absolute Positivity

Chapter **07**

Fivefold Positivity(5): Positive View of Future

> Visions and dreams are the language of God the Holy Spirit.
>
> **– Yong-gi Cho**

The last of the Fivefold positivity is the positive view of the future. Positive thinking about the future allows us to grow into a person with dreams and visions. God works as we dream. This is how important it is to have expectations for the future and what hopes and visions we have.

I first saw a black pastor when I was in 6th grade. This was when Yoido Full Gospel Church was in Seodaemun. I only saw white pastors like missionary John Hurston up to that point. It was amazing when I first saw a black pastor. At that time, I met the black pastor and followed him around and said, "the color of the mole on my arm and the color of the pastor's skin is similar. I will go to your country and preach the gospel later."

It's been a long time since then. In 1993, Pastor Yong-gi Cho held the "African Holy Spirit Crusade" in Kenya, and while I was praying in front of many people, God reminded me of the dream I had 27 years ago. "Didn't you say that you followed a black pastor in your childhood and said you'll preach the gospel in Africa? That dream came true today."

I forgot my childhood dream, but God didn't forget it. God remembered the words I had confessed to dreaming about my future and guided me to make that dream come true. Like this, it is important to dream in faith.

Miracle belongs to the one who anticipates

One of the ministers who had a great influence on Pastor Yong-gi Cho was Pastor Oral Roberts of the United States. The pastor stuttered in speech in the past, as a lung disease patient, he was cured and became an amazing minister. According to God's prophetic word, he even built Oral Roberts University. Pastor Roberts once published an autobiography that summarized the core principles of his ministry, the book was titled, *Expect a Miracle*. Having experienced miracles throughout his life, he was proving that miracles do not happen without expectation. If you trust and anticipate a good God who has amazing plans for your life, good things can happen and you can experience miracles.

> *What no eye has seen, what no ear has heard, and what no human mind has conceived — the things God has prepared for those who love him. _ 1 Corinthians 2:9*

The Dutch painter Vincent Van Gogh, who once wanted to become a priest, sent a letter to his younger brother Theo in 1888. "I can't help it even if my work doesn't sell. But one day people will find that my paintings are worth more than my life, than the paint I used for them." Today, Van Gogh's paintings are traded up to tens of billions of KRW, however, when he was painting, he had to suffer because he didn't have the necessary living expenses right away. He wasn't desperate. He believed that his paintings would one day be recognized by the world. He didn't get discouraged with a positive self-image about himself. God's man with positive faith should expect God's miracle. Helen Keller, who suffered three types disability of being unable to see, being unable to hear, and being unable to speak properly, said, “A person without expectations and dreams is a poor person.”

In spite of his illness, there was a boy who dreamt while looking at his future with positive eyes in the midst of prayer. Pastor Hyun -chul Cho of Orange Hill Presbyterian Church in the United States. Pastor Hyun-chul Cho was diagnosed with cerebral palsy at the age of one. He had to live with pain because of cerebral palsy that twisted his whole body, and he even had to twist his whole body to say a word.

Then he received Jesus when he was in middle school. After that, God’s grace came, and while reading the Bible and praying, he became a positive person who filled his future with positive dreams. The verse, “You raise the weak and shame the strong,” 1 Corinthians 1:27, touched his heart. ‘God will use me. God will be honored through me. I’ll be a pastor in the future. I be a revivalist as well as a pastor!’ This dream came into his mind and began to grow. People around him caustically called it a vain dream. “No, you can’t even control your body, but you have to twist your whole body to say a word, so how can you become a pastor?” His parents also tried to stopped him.

But he started dreaming of studying in the U.S., he put up an American map and prayed day and night with his hand on the map. "God, let me go to America to study and become a pastor!" God fulfilled that dream when he prayed with a positive attitude about his future. After graduating from seminary in Korea, he went to Azusa Pacific University in the U.S. and got a master's degree. And now, he became the first pastor with cerebral palsy and is doing ministry in a Korean Church in America.

He confesses. "For me, before I met Jesus, obstacles were obstacles to life. But after I met Jesus, I had a dream. I realized that disability is no longer a disability. Disability is no longer a stumbling block for me. Now I put my disability down before God. God, I want to give this obstacle to You. This disability will no longer be an obstacle for me, but a tool to reveal God's glory, and a channel of blessing to benefit God's church and family. God shames the strong through the weak."

Pastor Cho had a severe disability in his body, but he held onto the Word and prayed. In the midst of this life, he developed a positive faith and dream and experienced God's miracle.

You are God's dream

God is also a dreamer. What was God's dream? God said, "You will be for me a kingdom of priests and a holy nation,"Exodus 19:6 He had a dream for Israel, as His people. But God's true dream was Jesus Christ. God had a dream of saving mankind through Jesus. So he sent Jesus Christ to die on the cross, and He cleared the problem of our sins. He has opened the way for us to live by the power of the Holy Spirit, not by the wisdom and power of the weak. He healed our weaknesses and diseases. He has taken us from the curse and brought us blessings. He opened the way to heaven and eternal life for us. He made this wonderful blessing come to all those who believe in Jesus Christ, the son of God. Now each and every one of you is God's dream. God wants to fulfill his dream and mission through you.

It is said that two different horses run around in a person's mind. One is the black horse symbolizing despair and the other is the white horse symbolizing hope. The direction of life depends on which horse you feed the most. We need to feed the white horse in our hearts a lot so that we can run towards hope. When you feed the Word of God, you can move towards hope.

Henry Ford, the king of cars in the United States, didn't even attend elementary school. But he had a dream. It was one powerful asset that no one else had. He had a dream about the automobile business, looking at the wagon running, thinking, "can't we make a car that can go without a horse?" His wife's encouragement and faith were of great help, especially in his dream and realization. Eventually, he made a car that could go without a horse as he dreamt. This car would become the Ford Motor Company. After the couple died, people built a memorial hall and made an inscription, which read. "Ford was a person of dreams. His wife was a person of faith." Like this, dreams and faith are the best partners.

Dwight Lyman Moody said, "People in the world believe what they see, but believers see what they believe." When God wants to bless a person, he first instills a dream in his heart.

When I was working in Tokyo, Japan, there were many homeless people in Shinjuku Park in Tokyo. One day, I evangelized a homeless man in the park and brought him to church, he was originally a president of an electronics business. He graduated from a prestigious university and was good at English, but when the company went bankrupt, he became homeless because he wasn't able to face his family. Even if he was the boss in the past, he didn't look different from other homeless people because he'd been homeless for a long time

But his appearance started to change ever since he came to church. First, his eyes changed. At first, his eyes were empty without any motivation, but his eyes became clearer as he came to the service and listened to the Word. At some point, he began to worship on Sunday wearing clean clothes and a tie. Over time, the homeless figure disappeared and eventually became a completely different person. Later, when he heard the story, he thought, "I shouldn't live without any purpose like this," and gradually had a dream of recovering his daily life. It was the dream he had that changed him. He had a dream given by God, not a dream of the world. In this way, Christians should embrace the 'holy dream' given by God, not the ambition of the world.

Dreams and visions are signs of the Holy Spirit

Individuals, communities, and countries are doomed without dreams and visions. "Where there is no revelation, people cast off restraint; but blessed is the one who heeds wisdom's instruction." As proven by the words of Proverbs 29:18, the people who do not have the revelation and dream of God's Word will perish. However, if we are to receive God's dream and achieve it, we must be filled with the Holy Spirit. This is because when filled with the Holy Spirit, God's wisdom and ability comes to life and we are filled with God's vision and dreams. Receiving the Holy Spirit becomes a turning point in life and faith. It's not a life for me, but a life for the gospel of the Lord Acts 1:8.

The turning point of my life was the experience of the baptism of the Holy Spirit. At that time, I was only an elementary school graduate, but my religious life changed 180 degrees after the baptism of the Holy Spirit. Before receiving the Holy Spirit, I believed in Jesus only with my head. When I thought of Jesus, I was not moved deeply in my heart, and when I thought of Jesus' cross, I didn't shed a tear. But after receiving the Holy Spirit I began to feel overwhelmed by the emotion of God's love. For the next few years, I teared up just thinking about Jesus' cross.

When I became a class president in my first year of high school, I went to school an hour early every day and prayed for the class' salvation by calling the names of my classmates one by one. Also, I had a dream to give my whole life for the kingdom of God. I had faith that was positive that God will use me. Since receiving the Holy Spirit, I have never doubted God's love no matter what. If you want a great turning point in your life, you should be baptized by the Holy Spirit. You must adore and pray for the Holy Spirit.

The prophet Joel predicted that in the end days, when the Holy Spirit comes, "Your sons and daughters will prophesy, your old men will dream dreams, your young men will see visions." Joel 2:28 When the Holy Spirit comes, regardless of age or environment, you will dream God's dream. Believers who are full of the Holy Spirit will be guided by the Word of God and will have visions and dreams through the word of God. If you realize the word of God and the word gives you a vision in your life, it is that the Holy Spirit working in you. When the Holy Spirit comes, we'll have a vision to live for, thus living for the sake of the gospel of the Lord, not simply living the dream of eating and living well Acts 1:8.

Dreams of God revealed in the heart

God never works on a whim. He plans ahead and prepares. Even when guiding our lives, God prepares us, in our hearts.

For it is God who works in you to will and to act in order to fulfill his good purpose. _ Philippians 2:13

Here, 'will' means a dream. When we pray, God the Holy Spirit gives us holy desires in our hearts and makes us dream. Pastor Yong-gi Cho said, "Visions and dreams are the language of the Holy Spirit." Vision and dreams are more active when we pray in spirit because they are the language of the spirit. When we long for God's dream, God talks to us. He tells us where to go. It transcends reason, environment, and sense, to have God's dream.

"Your will be done on earth as it is in heaven." Matthew: 6:10, the Lord's Prayer, there is a prayer where the will must be done in heaven first to be done on earth. Pastor Yong-gi Cho said, "In the sky, there is more than the sky, there is also the sky in the heart of believers." This is because the Holy Spirit, the Spirit of God, makes the body and mind of the believer a temple. So when we pray, God's will becomes a revelation in the heart through the Holy Spirit, and the will is fulfilled in life.

When our faith becomes stronger and God's word is working in us, God's mission and dream works more powerfully in us. Therefore, our knowledge or educational background, our appearance or wealth do not guide our lives, but God's dream leads our lives. We study, we make money, we do business, we eat, we exercise, we do everything for God's vision and glory1 Corinthians 10:31.

Hardships and dreams are friends

Hardship is said to be friends with God's dreams. Sarah, Abraham's wife, wasn't able to get pregnant, which was in accordance with God's training curriculum. He trained her to persevere and to have faith in God's promise. Eventually, when Abraham was 100, he saw a miracle of receiving a son.

Joseph was hated by his brothers for his dream and had to go through an unspeakable journey of hardship. He was sold as a slave because of his dream, and he was falsely accused and imprisoned. Furthermore, he had to spend two years patiently in prison because the cupbearer, who was reinstated after interpreting his dream, completely forgot about him. But when the time came, God raised him and made him prime minister of Egypt. Joseph went through all kinds of hardships for 13 years before his dream came true. Like this, the results of dreams are beautiful, but the process of achieving them isn't serene. You don't have to be afraid of hardship. For a dreamer, hardship is a path of blessing for a dream to come true. The Bible records the facts as the following.

And he sent a man before them—Joseph, sold as a slave. They bruised his feet with shackles, his neck was put in irons, till what he

foretold came to pass, till the word of the LORD proved him true.
_ Psalm 105:17-19

The Bible says, "The word of God has disciplined him." Even in an environment where it is hard to believe in a dream, it is the process of making a dream come true.

God told Noah to make an ark before he judged the whole world with water. After making the ark with three floors, he told Noah to make a window about 45 to 50 centimeters long from the top of the ark's ceilingGenesis 6:16. Noah did not see the flood while the water was overflowing for 40 days because there was no window on the side. When he opened the window, he could only see the sky. God made Noah look only at the sky during the flood.

There is a saying, "All four sides are blocked, but the top is open." The sky is open. When we face hardships such as floods, we should only look at the sky, not at the environment that discourages and frightens us. We should only look to God's dreams and words.

Through hardship, we train to look at the sky and learn humility from it. If we are not trained in humility, it is easy to mistake God's dream as our own achievement because we think we're good.

However, those who have been humbled through hardship will give all the glory to God when their dreams come true. Let's believe in God's sovereignty and providence, persevering in the faith.

Visualize your dreams and pray specifically

To achieve your dream, you need to visualize it. Even if your dream hasn't come true yet, you should be able to picture your dream coming true. You have to keep drawing while looking at God's vision with the eyes of faith. When God trained Abraham's faith, he trained him to paint with faith. He made him look at the stars in the night sky, and he made him look at countless grains of sand on the beachGenesis 13:14-15, 15:5. Real faith is continuing to look at God's word and His promises in the seemingly impossible reality.

Pam Lontos, president of an American counseling company, was obese when she was young and slept for more than 18 hours a day. She always felt depressed and hopeless but at some point, her mind changed. 'I can't live like this. It must be changed,' she began to think, and from then on she listened to cassette tapes with positive messages all day. She started to say positive things about herself more than 50 times a day. 'I am a decent person. I am not defeated. 'I can do well, too,' she confessed. Further, she put a picture of a great actress on the wall, removed the actress' face from the picture, and attached her face on actress' neck. Seeing it, she laughed in content, and confessed, "I am like that person."

Curiously, at some point, changes began to appear. She started to lose weight. She was able to lose 20kg more when she tried a little harder. Since then, she has gained confidence and got a job as a salesperson, and even then, she worked by portraying herself as a sales queen every day. But after a while, she really became a sales queen. She didn't stop there, at that time she started to picture in her mind how she would sell things on TV.

Then one day, she went to Shamrock TV Station and asked for employment. However, she was rejected. They said, "Your character is so unattractive that we can't use it on our broadcast." Nevertheless, she continued to challenge herself, dreaming of joining the station. Eventually, she joined the company, and after two years, she became the vice president of the company as a result of having positive faith and dreams. After that, she established a counseling company and acted as president. She became a national celebrity in the U.S.

To achieve your dream, you have to keep looking at it with faith.

It's better to write down your dreams in detail and pray specifically. It is good to write down your personal dreams, dreams about your family, dreams related to your job, and watch them every day and pray.

When I was building a church in the United States, there was an American church member who donated three houses. He came to me one day and showed me his notebook. The notebook was filled with 84 prayer requests. Every morning, he opened his notebook and looked at the request of prayers from No. 1 to 84, saying, "No. 1, please fill me with the Holy Spirit! No. 2, please give me good health! Number three, bless my company!" he prayed. Surprisingly, when he looked back a year later, he testified that more than 60 of the prayer requests were answered. Then, instead of stopping there, he wrote down more than 80 new prayer requests in his notebook and prayed every day. God has a clear dream that he wants to achieve through us. You should keep that dream in mind, make a clear plan, and pray in detail.

Ancora Imparo

To achieve God's dream, you have to build up your skills, and what you need is humility. You can build up your skills when you are humble. A humble person knows his or her shortcomings and always has an attitude to learn.

Matsushita Konosuke is the founder of Panasonic in Matsushita Electric Industrial Prefecture in Japan. He once summarized three secrets of his success as an entrepreneur. "First, my secret to success is poverty. I was very poor, so I cleaned shoes, delivered newspapers, and had many hurtful experiences in life. Secondly, the secret of my success is my weakness. I suffered a lot of disabilities due to my weak body. In the end, I exercised hard for my health and did my best to build up my physical strength. Third, I couldn't even get out of elementary school properly. In the end, I read diligently to overcome the obstacle of being uneducated. I read a lot of books. Reading books nonstop has become a shortcut to overcoming the obstacles of being uneducated." His story is a great example of how he can sublimate his weaknesses into a journey of learning.

Pastor Yong-gi Cho also said, "Through the experience of poverty, I was able to hold a public pastoral meeting to know the hearts of the common people, study and pray about healing while suffering from many diseases, and read more and developed myself due to the lack of formal academic education." Rev. Billy Graham has also previously said, "I always try to learn, even at my age of mid-80s." All of these people have a constant attitude to learn without blaming their lack of opportunity. This is how important it is to overcome environmental constraints and learn and try.

There's a Latin word "Ancora Imparo." This is what Michelangelo Buonarroti, a genius artist, said. He painted the world-famous painting, *The Creation*, on the ceiling of the Sistine Chapel, with the Pope electing him at the age of 87. At 87 years of age, he painted the ceiling and left the word "Ancora Imparo," which means, "I'm still learning." It's a confession that showed that he doesn't know it all and that he's still learning.

There is a saying, "The leader is a life-time learner." We can learn from the people around us, and we can learn through our difficult conditions. You can learn by working at work, and you can learn from the Holy Spirit who is our teacher. But one of the effective ways to learn is to read.

To fulfill what you're called to do, you must value the habit of reading. You should read the Bible and read books in your field or specialty. If you read more than 50 books in one field, you can have some expertise in the field. I go to the bookstore several times a month to buy books and read them whenever I have time, gain new information, knowledge, and insights through reading. It is also good to take notes on important parts when reading a book. Singapore's Prime Minister Kuan Yew Lee once said, "Blurry ink lasts longer than clear memories." It emphasizes the importance of memo habits when reading. If you want to achieve your dream, you have to constantly read and learn.

The Bible describes Joseph through the lips of his brothers. What about you? Are you dreaming like Joseph?

Here comes that dreamer! They said to each other. _ Genesis 37:19

We should have God's dreams and visions with expectations for the future. If you pray with the Holy Spirit, God's holy hope will come true. Have a dream about your home. Dream of your child becoming an influential believer in the world. Have a holy dream that your business is blessed, that through your business you can support missions and save the poor. At the same time, dream of revival of the church. It will come true as you dream.

Positivity Quotient Check List ☑

Positive view of Future Quotient Check List?

Instructions: Please read each statement and select the most appropriate response to indicate how frequently you experience the behavior described in the statement.

Statements	Never	Rarely	Some times	Often	Always
	1	2	3	4	5
1. I believe that God has great expectations and plans for my life.					
2. I feel optimistic and hopeful about my future.					
3. I'm expecting God to give me a miracle in my life.					
4. When I pray in the Holy Spirit, I feel my holy desires will come true.					
5. The vision and dream that God gives me is passionately enflamed in my heart.					
6. When hardship comes my way, I persevere with the dream, the friend that God has given me.					
7. I always picture achieving my vision and my future.					
8. I write down my dream and pray specifically to achieve it.					
9. I am always studying and learning to achieve my dream.					
10. I am a missionary to fulfill God's dream and vision until I die.					

After reading each statement, check the corresponding box.
Add up the checked scores for each statement.

Totals (   ) points

The tongue has the power of life and death,
and those who love it will eat its fruit.

Proverbs 18:21

Chapter 08

Threefold Training(1): Proclamation of Positive Words

Chapter **08**

Threefold Training(1): Proclamation of Positive Words

> The words we speak become the house we live in.
>
> **– Hafiz**

I first attended Yoido Full Gospel Church in April 1964. There is a story that I heard from Pastor Yong-gi Cho during my attendance at the church. Every time he preached, he said, "Don't ever talk about negative things, folks. Don't say you can't live or die. Why do you say you're going to die? I'm starving. I'm so full. I'm dying of love. I'm going to die of evil. Why do you say you're going to die? Say I'm going to live. No negative words should be spoken. We have to say something positive and creative." At first, I laughed comfortably and listened to it, but at some point, I stopped saying negative things or complaining. The word permeated deep within my bone.

So far, we've looked at the Fivefold positivity. It is having a positive view of self, others, work and calling, environment, and future. The proclamation and training of positive language is important for the Fivefold positivity to be realized and be effective.

Pastor Yong-gi Cho said that words is the culmination of the Fourth dimension spirituality, which consists of the elements of thought, faith, dream, and words. Only when words change first, can we change ourselves, the environment, the sense of duty, and furthermore, others and the future. God created everything in the universe with words and made humans in His image. He gave us a language to communicate with humans who resemble the image of God. This allows us to use the power of God-given language. It is important to train and declare the language of positivity to bring upon absolute change in our lives because God gives us the fruit of life, as we say with our lips. "'Creating praise on their lips. Peace, peace, to those far and near,' says the LORD. 'And I will heal them.'"Isaiah 57:19

Positive words of encouragements people love to hear

Previously, the Seoul Metropolitan Office of Education investigated what students, parents, and teachers want to hear the most. At the time, it turned out that they wanted to hear the compliment, "Well done, you did a great job." Also, when the Chungcheongbuk-do Office of Education asked students what they wanted to hear the most, "you can do it" accounted for the highest percentage of the answers. This is also a reminder that everyone wants to hear words of encouragement and affirmation, "Well done, you can do it."

There was a boy born in the slums of Detroit. The boy was ostracized by white students at school because he was black. He was the last place in his class because he couldn't memorize the multiplication tables until he was in the 5th grade of elementary school. The boy later became the world's best doctor. He was the first person in the world to perform the separation surgery of Siamese twins. He became known as God's Hand, Dr. Ben Carson of Johns Hopkins University Hospital, Boleyn. It is said that he was able to open up that future because of what his mother said to him. "Ben, you can do anything if you want to. You can be anything if you try!" The Bible says, "From the fruit of their mouth a person's stomach is filled."Proverbs 18:20 The language of positivity renews us and allows us to look at the environment and the future anew.

There was a father who lost both arms in a high-voltage electric shock while working as an electrician. But one day, his four-year-old son came to his father and said, "Daddy, please draw for me." He said he wanted to listen to what his son said to him, so he tried to draw with a pen in his prosthetic hand. The child was very happy with the painting that his father drew, and the father of the child became interested in painting while drawing, so he learned to paint and became a painter. This is the true story of artist Chang-woo Seok, who pioneered a new genre called ink croquis. Every word of the child made a remarkable difference in the father's life.

There is also a saying in our proverb, "A kind word pays off a thousand coins of debt." This saying represents the positive power of words. There's also an old story related to this proverb. Once upon a time, there was a butcher, pujugan-means butcher in a marketplace. One day, two yangban upper class, came to buy meat. One of them made an order to the butcher without using honorifics. "Hey, give me a piece of meat." The butcher cut the meat and gave it to him. After that, another gentleman standing next to him ordered differently. "Mr. Kim, please give me a piece of meat." The butcher said, "Yes, I see," and cut the meat, but he gave him much more than the gentleman who bought the meat at first. The gentleman who bought the meat first shouted angrily. "Hey, we both asked for a pound of meat, but why is there such a difference?" The butcher said, "Your meat is cut by the butcher, and this meat is cut by Mr. Kim, so it has to be different."

Positive words reveal positive power not only in our future but also in our interpersonal relationships. The faith of positivity gives birth to the language of positivity, and the language of positivity makes our lives positive.

Negative words are infectious

In Yong-jin Jang's, *Communication of a Good Worker*, there is a saying. "The person bitten by a dog was treated and returned in half a day. The person bitten by a snake was treated and returned in three days. However, the person who was bitten by a person's words hasn't returned and is still hospitalized. This speaks to the negative power of language.

Even in the Talmud, negative gossip about others will kill three people. The person who spreads the gossip, the person who is listening without opposing it, and the main person of the gossip.

EBS Knowledge Channelⓔ once aired a video called *Retaliation of a Curse*. The video features an experiment in which participants are told to remember and write down 12 words from 4 different categories. Each category contains 3 words and the words presented are positive, negative, forbidden, and neutral. The participants tried to remember each word well, but as soon as the forbidden word appeared, they forgot the previous words. According to the video, the language of swearing is remembered four times stronger than other words, and it strongly stimulates the brain with emotions that make you feel anger or fear, preventing the brain activity of thinking logically. When people were asked why they used abusive language, they said 25.7% said it became a habit, 18.2% said it was used by others, and 17.0% said it was to relieve stress through words. This experiment clearly shows how much people are affected by negative language.

The people of Israel chose 12 spies from Kadesh Barnea in the desert. They were about to enter Canaan and sent them to spy. However, they were completely discouraged by the negative words spoken by ten spies except Joshua and CalebNumbers 14:1-4. All of the

Israel people were infected by negative words and cried in despair and blamed the leaders, Moses and Aaron. In fact, these negative words and resentments were against God who saved them from Egypt. So God said, "As surely as I live, declares the LORD, I will do to you the very thing I heard you say."Numbers 14:28 He will repay them as they say negatively, as they complain and grumble. In the end, only Joshua and Caleb were able to enter Canaan and the rest died in the wilderness. "The tongue has the power of life and death, and those who love it will eat its fruit."Proverbs 18:21

We shouldn't be infected by negative words. Don't say negative things, don't listen, and don't transfer them. Negative words limit God's work. We need to remember that Jesus was also the son of God, but he could not perform healing ministry and miracles in his hometown of Nazareth.

> *Jesus said to them, "A prophet is not without honor except in his own town, among his relatives and in his own home." He could not do any miracles there, except lay his hands on a few sick people and heal them. He was amazed at their lack of faith. _ Mark 6:4-6*

The Bible records that Jesus "couldn't perform any power." It was because of the distrust and negative words of the people back home. "'Isn't this the carpenter, Isn't this Mary's son and the brother of James, Joseph, Judas and Simon? Aren't his sisters here with us?' And they took offense at him."Mark 6:3 Even though Jesus, the son of God, came there himself, the people missed the opportunity of grace, love, and miracles. It's a pity.

The same goes for us. Even if the great Lord comes among us, if we think negatively and speak negatively, we cannot experience any grace or miracle. Negative thoughts give rise to negative words. Negative faith give rise to negative words, and negative words block God's miracle and darken our future.

Power of uplifting words

The word of God is 'a word that always saves.' God created the world through words. The world was created by God's word and was beautiful and goodGenesis 1:31. When God created Eve, she would be his helper, Adam lifted his voice, "This is now bone of my bones and flesh of my flesh,"Genesis 2:23 in the language of positivity and love.

However, after committing a crime, the beautiful language of positivity changed into a negative language that hides one's sins, smears others, and covers up one's mistakes.

> *The man said, "The woman you put here with me—she gave me some fruit from the tree, and I ate it." Then the LORD God said to the woman, "What is this you have done?" The woman said, "The serpent deceived me, and I ate." _ Genesis 3:12-13*

Since the fall, mankind has destroyed the world and destroyed human relationships through constant negative words and words that kill. But our good God sent His only son Jesus and began to heal the world full of negative language.

Jesus is a man whose words have become fleshJohn 1:1, 14. Jesus, the word of God, delivered the blessed news to the people wherever he went. He healed and saved people. He went to the tomb of Lazarus, who had been dead for four days and shouted, "Lazarus Come out"John 11:43 and the dead Lazarus came back to life.

Jesus' words are words that save. It's a word that wins over the power of death. If we follow Jesus and want to resemble him, we should use words that saves others, not negative words that kill.

Tommy and Jimmy are brothers who lived at St. Joseph's

Orphanage in Jackson, Michigan, in the United States. When his older brother Jimmy became a middle school student, he followed his adoptive parents and they had no choice but to break up. His younger brother, Tommy, also became a middle school student under his adoptive parents, but he became a problem child and eventually was expelled from school. However, when he left the school gate, he suddenly remembered the words of Sister Verada, who coached him at the orphanage. "God never abandons you. Try hard to get a big star." Tommy took courage and got a job at a pizza store, and learned an amazing skill in kneading a pizza in 11 seconds. Later, he established Domino's Pizza, the second largest pizza chain in the United States today. Domino's Pizza founder Thomas Monaghan was once a troublemaker, even expelled from school.

The Bible says, "If anyone speaks, they should do so as one who speaks the very words of God."1 Peter 4:11 Every word I say can give courage and hope to others. Whatever you say, you have to say something that encourages and saves others. In order to say words that give life, we must adore and be filled with the Holy Spirit and internalize the positive words of God.

Your language changes when the Holy Spirit comes

Using the language of positive faith words isn't simply by human will or effort. You must seek the help of the Holy Spirit. We must desperately seek to be filled with the Holy Spirit. "Be filled with the Spirit." Ephesians 5:18 The Greek language of the word is passive and present tense. The Holy Spirit fills me, I don't fill the Holy Spirit. The reason why a person who has been filled with the Holy Spirit makes a mistake is that the grace of the Holy Spirit has cooled, that is, the 'fire' has cooled.

When I was a pastor in the United States, there was an elder named Dong-ho Ahn. He was a former surgeon at Kei-Myung University. He always told me, "Pastor, don't wait until the car fuel goes down to empty. Always fill it up when it goes down a little bit from the middle. If it goes down to empty, you may be in trouble later." However, I forgot because I didn't pay attention to it even after hearing it. And one day, I went to the atrium far away and ran out of fuel, and the car stopped. I couldn't help but feel embarrassed when I suddenly stood on the side of the road. Fortunately, I was able to run to the gas station having the car parked on the side of the road, thankfully it wasn't on the highway, and returned with gasoline in a container and filled the car with some gas.

Even if we receive the Holy Spirit, this can happen when the fire is extinguished and the grace is cooled. You can stop on the path of grace and be frustrated. You can commit crimes and make mistakes. One of the ways we can tell whether we're full of the Holy Spirit is to look at the words we use in life. When the grace of the Holy Spirit cools, many negative words, words of despair, words of resentment, and words of complaint come out of our mouths. However, when we are filled with the Holy Spirit, words of praise and gratitude overflow.

Do not get drunk on wine, which leads to debauchery. Instead, be filled with the Spirit, speaking to one another with psalms, hymns, and songs from the Spirit. Sing and make music from your heart to the Lord. _ Ephesians 5:18-19

In order for positive words, words of praise and gratitude, and words of vision to come out of our mouths, we must adore and pray to be filled with the Holy Spirit. Furthermore, it is important to put the Word of God in our hearts and on our lips.

Internalize the Word of God

God is the God of absolute positivity, so God's words are always positive. When we read, meditate, recite, and internalize the words, we can change into positive people of faith. The Bible orders the Word of God to be engraved on our hearts.

My son, keep my words and store up my commands within you. Keep my commands and you will live; guard my teachings as the apple of your eye. Bind them on your fingers; write them on the tablet of your heart. _ Proverbs 7:1-3

Engrave is a word used to carve letters on things like stone or iron. To engrave God's word on our heart means to keep God's word deeply engraved on our hearts of stone so we remember it. In order to allow words to enter a negative and hardened heart, you must engrave them powerfully as if you were engraving them on a monument. Human memory can easily be lost, so it also means to engrave words like engraving them on a stone so that you don't forget them.

Biblical meditation and recitation are effective ways to internalize the word of God in this respect. One psychologist said, "A person's memory is limited. If you just listen to a story, you will remember only 8% after 24 hours, but if you listen to it while recording it in your notebook, 25% is remembered and if you review it while thinking about it carefully, 58% is remembered, and almost everything you recited can be remembered." When negative thoughts come to mind or as we face difficult situations, meditating and reciting God's words of positivity allows us to control negative emotions and language and do as God wants.

Jeremiah Denton of the United States, was a prisoner of the Vietnam War for seven years. He spent most of his seven years in solitary confinement and was tortured to the point of passing out. However, he was later released and survived and was elected to the U.S. Senate of Alabama.

How could Denton overcome the anguish and solitary confinement of his captivity? He chose to recite the Word as the reason for his survival. He meditated and thought about the Word of God he was reciting. Thus, despite the pain of torture and persecution, he overcame it all with the Word of God. It was his spiritual weapon to reflect on the words and meditate. By meditating on God's Word, God spoke to him and gripped him in His grace. He was able to overcome all difficulties, and the Bible recitation verses became his prayer. When we think and pray on the word of God in this way, the anxiety and fear in our hearts will disappear and the faith of positivity will arise.

Power of proclamation

Jesus looked at the fig tree as he went up to the temple of Jerusalem. But when the tree had no fruit, He cursed it. "Then he said to the tree, 'May no one ever eat fruit from you again.' And his disciples heard him say it."Mark 11:14 Here we must know that Jesus spoke to the tree. As Jesus said, the fig tree was cursed and could not bear fruit.

Everything that exists in this world is governed by the power of what the people of faith say. Joshua ordered the sun to stopJoshua 10:12, and Jesus also ordered the waves and the wind to be stillMark 4:39. We too can pray and command our body, about the disease, about our situation and even about the future.

Methodist Missionary Stanley Jones, a well-known Indian missionary, collapsed from a stroke at the age of 69. He went to the U.S. to get treatment, and all the doctors said, "He's old, His cerebrovascular erupted, and because of his stroke, he won't be able to get up again." But the missionary believed in the ability of positive and active speech. He asked the nurses and doctors who came into the room to say the following. "Don't say good morning when you come in in the morning or good night in the evening. Instead, when you come in the morning or evening, declare to me 'Stanley Jones, in the name of Jesus, get up!'"

When they answered, "Missionary, how can you say such a thing when we are not even ministers?" The missionary became angry and said, "If you don't say so, I'll be discharged from this hospital." Inevitably, the doctors and nurses said, "Stanley, get up. Rise and shine in the name of Jesus!" And then something amazing happened. All the doctors that said the missionary would not be able to get up, kept saying, "I order you in the name of Jesus, get up." And then he went back to India, and after 20 more years of missionary work, he went to heaven. Amazing abilities and miracles appear when you believe and proclaim the positive word of God.

If any of you are sick, hold onto the Bible about healing and declare it with your name. "Because of Jesus' stripes, I, ____ am healed."Isaiah 53:5 If there is a heavy burden in your life, declare your name in the following phrase. "Come to me, all you who are weary and burdened ____, and I will give you rest ____."Matthew 11:28

In this way, recite and meditate on the appropriate Word of God, declare His name, and pray. It's effective.

Make a habit of proclaiming positive words

According to a paper published by researchers at Duke University in the United States, 40 percent of the choices we repeat every day are determined by habits, not by careful decision-making processes. Psychologist William James also said, "Our lives are made up of habit blocks." Charles Duhigg, a New York Times reporter, says in a book called, *The Power of Habits*. "The core habit is important. When core habits begin to change, other habits can be changed and modified as well... Also, willpower is a habit. Willpower is not just a skill, but similar to the muscles of the arms or legs, so if you use it a lot, you get tired... So, if you have willpower in your core habits, you can make effective habits."

Pastor Rick Warren of Saddleback Church also spoke about the importance of spiritual training and habits. "If you force people to copy Christ, you might be able to have them follow temporarily, but it doesn't work in the long run. The only way to make spiritual maturity a responsibility of oneself is to teach how to habituate faith. From the moment faith becomes a habit, they move on their own."

Putting the words above together, it is very important to have a spiritual will and create a core faith habit. Praying in admiration and being filled with the Holy Spirit, reading, meditating, reciting, and internalizing God's Word every day, and proclaiming the positive Word of God that gives strength in faith, these should be made key habits. When we wake up in the morning, which is also the key to the day, and when we fall asleep in the evening, which is the lock of the day, if we have this habit and practice it, a miracle of absolute positivity will happen to us all.

Examples of positive words of encouragement

Positive language declaration sample sentence. The next declaration is an example. Create a declaration that suits you and proclaim words of positivity in the name of Jesus Christ.

A declaration of affirmation of oneself

- I am a child who is loved by God!
- I am worthy, beautiful, precious, and chosen by God!
- All anxiety and worries shall be gone, and the peace of heaven shall come!
- All my weakness will be gone and I will be strengthened!
- May all my prayer requests be answered!
- Good things will happen today and it will be a day of joy and blessings!
- Many will be blessed through me!

A declaration of affirmation of others

- Peace and good health to your parents!
- May the faith of my spouse and children grow and may I be a source of blessing!
- You will say words of encouragement and praise to the people you meet today as well!
- There will be more people who support and encourage me!
- Be kind to the people you meet today!
- You will embrace and forgive others today as well!
- When you talk today, you'll say something positive!

Examples of positive words of encouragement

A declaration of work and mission

- I will realize God's calling through my workplace!
- God's kingdom and grace will come to my workplace!
- May your colleagues at work believe in Jesus and be saved!
- Evil spirit that interferes with my work get out!
- I hope you will work with joy today as well!
- You will work passionately and diligently today as well!
- Everything you plan and push ahead with will work!

A declaration of affirmation on a matter

- You will realize God's providence through your problems!
- Every barrier in life will be penetrated!
- May my acquaintance's disease be cured!
- Financial problems will be solved and breakthroughs will occur!
- May interpersonal conflict be resolved and blessings be upon you!
- You will learn patience and humility among your problems!
- All hardships and difficulties will work together to for good!

A declaration of affirmation to the church

- May all the services, hymns and prayers of our church be passionate and full of grace!
- May the senior pastor be filled with the Holy Spirit, inspiration and vision be with the sermon!
- Let all pastors serve the church with humility, sincerity and love!
- Spiritual revival will come to the hearts of the believers!

Examples of positive words of encouragement

- The church members will be united in the Lord!
- The church members will evangelize and the church will be revived!
- It will be a church that only reveals the glory of God!

A declaration of affirmation for the future

- My future will be full of expectations and hope!
- All obstacles and the devil in my way shall be gone!
- When I pray, I will be filled with the Holy Spirit and have a holy desire!
- I will picture dreams and visions and pray in detail!
- A coworker will come to fulfill God's dream!
- Let everything in my path be united to work together for good!
- May all the visions that God planned for my life be fulfilled!

Positivity Quotient Check List ☑

Proclamation of Positive Words Quotient Check List?

Instructions: Please read each statement and select the most appropriate response to indicate how frequently you experience the behavior described in the statement.

Statements	Never	Rarely	Some times	Often	Always
	1	2	3	4	5
1. Negative words never come out of my mouth.					
2. I often say words of encouragement and praise to others.					
3. I think positively of myself. I bless and declare.					
4. I believe that unbelief and negative words can distract from God's work and miracles.					
5. I often say words of blessings to others.					
6. I always read and meditate on God's Word.					
7. I pray by reciting the Word of God using it in appropriate situations.					
8. I give hope and words of life to others.					
9. I record God's vision and declare it whenever I have time.					
10. I believe there is power in words of faith. I declare and command diseases and problems to be healed and solved.					

After reading each statement, check the corresponding box.
Add up the checked scores for each statement.

Totals (   ) points

Give thanks in all circumstances;
for this is God's will for you
in Christ Jesus.

1 Thessalonians 5:18

Chapter 09

Threefold Training(2): Absolute Gratitude

Chapter **09**

Threefold Training(2): Absolute Gratitude

> God has two dwellings; one in heaven,
> And the other in a meek and thankful heart.
>
> **- Izaak Walton**

I visited the house of Deacon Kang, who attended our church. As soon as I entered the single room where the deacon, who was about 90 years old, lived alone, a savory smell greeted my group. The deacon prepared roasted sweet potatoes himself because he thought he should serve something when the senior pastor would visit. I always tell you not to prepare anything but I couldn't help but take the roasted sweet potatoes the deacon served with care that day. On that day, I delivered the words of Psalms 23 and talked with him while eating the most delicious roasted sweet potatoes in the world.

From man's perspective, the deacon's situation wasn't good. However, the deacon offered a carefully prepared thanksgiving offering, saying that he was truly grateful that he was living in peace with the grace of Jesus. When I saw the deacon, who lived alone in a single room but did not lose the joy of gratitude, I realized once again where gratitude came from. Appreciation didn't come from a bountiful setting, but a heart that served the Lord. If the Lord lives in your heart, the peace of heaven will come. If you live in peace, you will be able to express your gratitude in the mountains, in the rough fields, in the tents, in the palace, wherever you are.

Gratitude is the key to happiness

The head of Life Without Limbs, which serves as an organization for the physically disabled while preaching the gospel around the world, is Rev. Nick Vujicic of Australia. Born to a pastor father and a nurse mother, all the nurses cried when he was born without arms and right leg except for his short left foot due to a disease called "Sunrise Phocomelia." They advised his parents to give up their child and leave him to the facilities for the disabled but his parents didn't give up. As a child, he was bullied by children and fell into severe depression, and even thought of suicide at the age of eight. But the love of his family and his meeting with God changed his life.

Instead of focusing on what he didn't have, he began to focus on what he did have and appreciate it. He has engaged in various challenging activities such as golf, swimming, surfing, and horseback riding without being limited to disabilities, and he is still continuously challenging them. He confesses, "We wonder when we can be happy. But happiness has already begun when I am grateful for the things I have here now."

Mi-young Lee, Man-seok Kim, and Byung-wook Kim, the authors of the book *Management is Fun When You Meet Gratitude*, created the following with the acronym for the word "HAPPY."

H – Habit

A – Appreciation

P – Pleasure

P – Present

Y – Yourself

To sum up, happiness is the expression of 'how you're having fun now and habits of thankfulness.' No matter how good our lives may be, if we are not grateful, happiness will be far removed from us. However, if we can be thankful even in difficulty and difficult situations, our lives become happy. We must therefore be thankful under any circumstance, under any condition. You must live a life of gratitude to God for everything like Paul's recommendation1 Thessalonians 5:18.

Give thanks. 'Now.' Train yourself to discover things you can be grateful for under any circumstance. When we are grateful, our lives can be truly blessed, successful, and happy.

Is it a prison? Or a monastery?

In the book, *God Is Inescapable* by Dr. David Soper, a criminal psychologist, tells a story.

"Basically, the difference between a prison and a monastery is the difference between complaining and giving thanks. This is a definite fact. Prisoners in prison always complain when they are awake. On the other hand, the saints who voluntarily lock themselves in a monastery thank God whenever they are awake. If prisoners become saints through gratitude, the inside of the prison will become a monastery, and when the saints give up gratitude, the monastery will become a prison."

It's an amazing insight. Prisons and monasteries are not much different in terms of their life. But one place is full of complaint and resentment, and the other is full of joy and gratitude. Like this, no matter where we are, no matter what situation we encounter, we can live like prisoners or like saints, depending on what our minds are like. When I live with gratitude to God's love for me, Jesus' cross that turned my negative into positive, and the Holy Spirit who is always with me and helps me with His power will allow me to live with gratitude. The place where I dwell becomes a sanctuary and my life will be the life of a saint.

The Bible tells the story of people who opened the prison gates by singing hymns of thanksgiving. Paul and Silas were severely beaten and thrown into prison with shackles on their feet for driving out the evil spirit of a slave girl who had been fortune telling while they were preaching the gospel. But Paul and Silas did not complain or resent God. They didn't hate or curse those who hurt them. Rather, they prayed to God and praised Him, and their praise was heard by other prisoners. What happened next?

> *About midnight Paul and Silas were praying and singing hymns to God, and the other prisoners were listening to them. Suddenly there was such a violent earthquake that the foundations of the prison were shaken. At once all the prison doors flew open, and everyone's*

chains came loose. _Acts 16:25-26

When Paul and Silas prayed and praised, the gates of the prison opened, and the prisoners were freed from everything they'd been tied to. The guard who guarded Paul and Silas invited them to his house where he accepted Jesus Christ with repentance. And it's assumed, the Church of Philippi was established. The prison collapsed, and the sanctuary of the church of God was built. The kingdom of God came to Philippi due to Paul and Silas' faith of absolute positivity and gratitude for a God who is absolutely positive.

When faith of absolute positivity is expressed in gratitude

Thessalonica was the capital of the Roman Empire's Macedonia, an important port city at the heart of a sea route, but also the political and economic center where the Romans built Egnatia Street to run through. Marcus Tullius Cicero, a Roman politician who was once exiled there, referred to Thessalonica as the 'heart of our territory.'

When Paul saw the vision that of the Macedonians asking for help, he went to Thessalonica and preached the gospel to the Jews and the Gentiles who lived there. The Jews who were jealous of him caused a riot so he went to Berea but the believers of Thessalonica remained steadfast in all persecution and distress2 Thessalonians 1:3-4. Then Paul recommended to the church, where faith was established not too long ago, the believers in the midst of hardship were told to be "thankful in all circumstances." He said that it was God's will to be grateful not only for the gentiles but also for their country people as well. 'Regardless of the situation, no matter what happens,' "Give thanks in all circumstances; for this is God's will for you in Christ Jesus."1 Thessalonians 5:18

Talmud records the story of Akiva, one of the respected rabbis. One day, Akiva went a long way and took with him a lamp to read a book, a rooster to tell the time, a donkey to travel the long way, and a Torah, the scripture in Judaism. As it was getting dark, he went into a village and asked if he could stay overnight, but no one accepted him. He became homeless on the street, thinking, 'God will do something more favorable.' He couldn't fall asleep easily, so he turned on the light to read the Torah, but the wind blew it out. This time again, he thought, 'God will do something more favorable.' As he went back to sleep, he heard the cry of a fox, and the donkey and the rooster, surprised by the sound, and ran away. Now all he had left was the Torah. Nevertheless, he was thankful, saying, 'God will do something more favorable.' The next morning, after dawn, he could not help but be surprised as he entered the village. The night before, everyone in the house that had its light on was killed by a band of bandits. He found out that God had protected him.

There are many people who say, "I'll be thankful if there's something to be thankful for." But when I confess my gratitude with faith of absolute positivity, joy rises in my heart and the grace of the Lord overflows. The complicated problems that entangle me are solved at some point. Even if I can't understand why it came to me at the place, if I trust and appreciate God of absolute positivity, amazing things come in God's time and in God's way. Expressing the faith of absolute positivity through gratitude will change hardships into a blessing, sadness into joy, and experiencing the grace of despair turning into hope.

Testimony of gratitude that overcame terminal illness

I remember being very blessed after hearing the testimony of Pastor Byung-hee Yang of Yeongan Presbyterian Church. A sister in the church had cancer in the tongue and the doctor said all of her tongue had to be removed. She was hospitalized for surgery, and the whole family gathered the day before the surgery. When she would enter the operating room the next day, her tongue would be gone, and she wouldn't be able to speak for the rest of her life. Everyone was waiting with a heavy heart for the last words of the sister, then she started singing Hymn 511.

More love to Thee, O Christ, More love to Thee!
Hear Thou the prayer I make, On bended knee;

After completing the praise, she prayed with thanksgiving. "Thank you, Father God. I'm grateful that a sinner like me was saved and became a child of God. I am grateful for the Lord's peace and joy in my heart."

The next day, the operation began. But the doctor didn't start the procedure, he started a thorough examination again. And the tests showed that the tumor that had spread over itself to the tip of the tongue and the removal of just the tip would be sufficient. God heard the sister's confession of gratitude. Instead of pouring out anger and resentment, her praise of God's grace who saved her and her confession of absolute positivity brought upon a miracle.

4 Steps of Gratitude Training

A life of gratitude doesn't come overnight. According to the book *Management is Fun When You Meet Gratitude*, you go through four stages until you live a grateful life.

The first step is the 'stage of unconsciously complaining.' Most of us live complaining unconsciously. We know that gratitude is good, but out of habit complaining comes out naturally. However, if you decide to practice gratitude on occasion, you move on to the second step, the 'stage of thank you but complaining.' This is a stage where gratitude and dissatisfaction coexist. Next, the third step is the 'stage of conscious gratitude.' It is a stage where you refrain from thinking and saying things that are full of complaint, consciously thinking of gratitude, and furthermore, say words of gratitude. Once conscious gratitude has been trained, it is now the last step. You get to the stage of being grateful even if you're unaware of it. From this point on, you're always grateful and use words of gratitude.

What stage are you in right now? To live a life of "Being thankful in all circumstances," you need constant training of gratitude. I would like to share some guidelines with you to take you to a higher level of gratitude.

Gratitude Training: Perceiving the world with positive eyes

There is a saying, "If you don't live as you think, you will think as you live." The same is true of gratitude. Depending on what perspective we look at life and how we act, our lives can be full of things to be grateful for or things to complain about.

In some parts of South America, there is a place where cold and hot springs rise side by side. Hot water rises on one side and cold water flows next to it, and residents bring laundry, boil it in the hot spring, and rinse it in the cold spring. A tourist who saw the scene with an amazed look asked, "You must be grateful to God for giving you a hot spring and a cold spring in one place every time you wash your laundry?" The guide replied, "Not really. People here complain, 'How nice it would've been if we were given soap!'"

It sounds like a funny story, but if you think about it, we often are no different than them. We should always train to look at the world with positive eyes. I must believe that the God of absolute positivity is with me. Not only should you be grateful for the good things, but you should also be grateful by trusting God who will make good of the bad things. Instead of focusing on what you don't have, you should focus on what you have. Don't be discouraged by what you can't do, rather try to do what you can.

Gratitude Training: Let gratitude become a habit

You have to make gratitude a habit. The beginning of my day begins with 'thank you.' Every morning, I wake up and shout, "Thank you, God" more than 10 times. When I think of God's grace, I can't help but thank Him every moment of every day.

The famous New Testament scholar Rev. William B. Barclay, says in his book, *The Secret of Content*, and gives the following warning.

"Grumbling and complaining do not suit us as children of God. Unbelievers are fundamentally dissatisfied people, who have a thirst that can never be satisfied in this world. Therefore, grumbling makes us like the people who belong to this world, not the chosen people from this world. The unbeliever complains because he focuses on himself, but the true witness of Jesus Christ does not complain because he focuses on Jesus Christ."

Christian faith is faith of absolute positivity centered on the faith of the cross. There is no negative element in the gospel of our Christ, none whatsoever. Our gospel is the whole gospel. It's an absolute positive message to us all. The cross turned death into life, sorrow into joy, and curse into blessing. Therefore, we should be the ones who look at the cross of Jesus and confess our gratitude, even if there is nothing visible, nothing in our hands. "Strengthened in the faith as you were taught, and overflowing with thankfulness." Colossians 2:7

Keeping a Thank You Journal can be a good training method to make a habit of gratitude. I published a book called *Thank You QT 365* in our church so that all the church members can meditate on the Word and write down what they're grateful for every day. Even if it's a small thing, you can find something to be thankful about and write it down in the journal, where you can form a habit of gratitude.

Gratitude Training: Produce co-workers of gratitude

Missionary Kwang-kyu Choi, who wrote the book *God Above Everything*, went to the Dominican Republic as the first Korean in 1988 and established eight churches, including an elementary, middle, and high school. At Canaan Church, where the missionary works, up to 3,000 Sunday school students gather to worship God.

One day, the missionary went to a slum on the beach to deliver a message. Since more than 20 typhoons pass through this area every year, typhoons often came back and sweeping away everything as soon as houses and buildings that have collapsed have been restored. Due to economic difficulties as well as continued damages, residents were forced to fall into despair and discouragement.

While the missionary was praying for them, God said, "Make prayer warriors and pray. I will listen to your prayers." So, the missionary recruited seven thousand prayer warriors. This news spread throughout the Dominican Republic and also throughout the United States, and the country officially recognized the prayer warriors. In October 2009, 7,000 prayer warriors gathered and began to pray. At that time, pastors from Korea joined the prayer warriors and prayed with one heart, "Thanking God, they prayed to overcome the hurricanes," and an amazing miracle happened. In 2009, the Hurricane Headquarters in Miami predicted a total of 21 hurricanes, all of them after the ninth hurricane, 'Ida,' were wiped out.

When people of faith pray together, God works. You can't do

it alone, but you can achieve it if you work together. The same is true of gratitude. It is not easy for us to live a life of gratitude alone. We need gratitude warriors. It's also good for your family to begin a grateful life. It is recommended to create a partner to share confessions of gratitude at our workplace, business, or cell/district meeting. Sharing a grateful experience every week or month will be a great encouragement and comfort to one another. And there will be much more things to be thankful for.

Gratitude Training: Proclaim Thanksgiving daily

An attitude of positivity should lead to a confession of positivity, and an attitude of gratitude should come out as a confession of gratitude. Reverend Edward M. Bounds says, in *The Complete Works of E. M. Bounds on Prayer*,

> *"Faith makes up the impossible. Because faith allows God to work for us, and he is omnipotent. There are no limits to the ability of faith. If we drive out doubts from our hearts and expel distrust, what we ask of God will surely come true. God allows all that he has said to those who have faith."*

Positive faith and words affect our bodies and minds. Even words uttered habitually without thinking are input into the brain through the auditory organ, which changes our bodies and minds. Jong-min Woo, a professor of psychiatry at Seoul Paik Hospital, says, "The psychology contained in what we say habitually is reflected in our bodies and minds."

Therefore, we must not only believe with our hearts, but also confess with our mouthsRomans 10:10. Looking at the God of absolute positivity, we must believe with our hearts that he will work together all things for good. We must confess with our lips. When the declaration of the faith of gratitude is heard in our ears and heard in God's ears, our bodies and minds will be renewed and God's power will come upon our lives.

Examples of Thanksgiving Proclamation

The next declaration is an example. Make a declaration appropriate for each person, and say, "In the name of Jesus." Declare being grateful every day.

Gratitude for oneself

- Thank you for making me a child of God!
- Thank you for calling me for the kingdom of God!
- Thank you for answering my prayers and pleas!
- Thank you for making me strong!
- Thank you for working together to make all things good in my life!
- Thank you for allowing me to do well and have a peaceful day!
- Thank you for using me as a channel of blessing!

Gratitude for others

- Thank you for giving my parents peace and good health!
- Thank you for bringing my whole family together in faith!
- Thank you for letting me bless the people I meet today!
- Thank you for allowing me to share Your love!
- Thank you for letting me embrace and forgive others today!
- Thank you for allowing me to serve my neighbor with kind words and with helping hands!
- Thank you for letting me share what I'm thankful for!

Gratitude of work

- Thank you for letting the kingdom of God come to my workplace!

Examples of Thanksgiving Proclamation

- Thank you for letting what I do be God's joy!
- Thank you for letting me preach the gospel to my colleagues I work with!
- Thank you for letting the evil powers that interfere with my work and my calling leave!
- Thank you for allowing me to work with joy today!
- Thank you for allowing me to do everything as I'm doing for you Lord!
- Thank you for your kindness!

Gratitude towards our problems

- Thank you for making me realize God's will and wisdom through problems!
- Thank you for letting me meet someone to help me in the midst of the problem!
- Thank you for opening the way in the midst of the problem!
- Thank you God for solving my financial problems and blessing me!
- Thank you for helping me to resolve interpersonal conflicts!
- Thank you for letting me learn patience and humility in the midst of the problem!
- Thank you for all the hardships and difficulties to make good in my life!

Gratitude for the church

- Thank you for making our church a place where You are pleased!
- Thank you for the working of the Holy Spirit among all services, hymns, and prayers!

Examples of Thanksgiving Proclamation

- Thank you for giving me holy dreams and visions through our senior pastor!
- Thank you for allowing the pastors and the staff to serve the church with humility!
- Thank you for making all our church members adore the Word and the Holy Spirit!
- Thank you for lay leaders and church members be united together!
- Thank you for the passion of evangelism and for bringing our church to life!

Gratitude for the future

- Thank you for giving me holy dreams and visions!
- Thank you for making me dream of a blessed future!
- Thank you for destroying all the obstacles and devices that Satan laid in my way!
- Thank you for letting me picture dreams and visions and allowing me to pray specifically!
- Thank you for letting me meet my fellow co-workers to fulfill God's dream!
- Thank you for showing me that God is with me wherever I go!
- Thank you for allowing me to believe that all of God's dreams and desires for me will come true!

Positivity Quotient Check List

Absolute Gratitude Quotient Check List?

Instructions: Please read each statement and select the most appropriate response to indicate how frequently you experience the behavior described in the statement.

Statements	Never	Rarely	Some times	Often	Always
	1	2	3	4	5
1. I confess my gratitude to God when I wake up in the morning.					
2. I look for something to be thankful for even the smallest things in my daily life.					
3. I often express my gratitude to people around me.					
4. I am grateful and pray even if there is no immediate response to my prayer.					
5. I confess my gratitude rather than my complaints even if something difficult happens.					
6. I don't complain about what I don't have, but rather, give thanks for what I do have.					
7. I meditate on God's grace by writing in my thank you journal every day.					
8. I believe that hardships and problems are opportunities for faith and growth of character. I give thanks.					
9. I believe that God will make things for good even if things don't go the way I planned. I give thanks.					
10. I end each day with a prayer of thanksgiving before going to bed.					

After reading each statement, check the corresponding box.
Add up the checked scores for each statement.

Totals (   ) points

Give, and it will be given to you.
A good measure, pressed down,
shaken together and running over,
will be poured into your lap.
For with the measure you use,
it will be measured to you.

Luke 6:38

Chapter 10

Threefold Training(3): Sharing Love

Chapter **10**

Threefold Training(3): Sharing Love

> We make a living by what we get,
> But we make a life by what we give.
>
> **– Winston Churchill**

When I was young, I lived in Sangdo-dong, Seoul. At that time, everyone lived in poverty after the Korean War, and my grandfather used to climb the mountain behind Sangdo-dong every night. He didn't just climb up, but he put rice in a bag and sewed the opening of the bag with a sewing machine and carried it on his shoulder. After a while, my grandfather, who returned empty, went out carrying another bag of rice and climbed the mountain several times late at night. He secretly brought food to those who lived in the mountains without homes.

What's interesting is that the people who lived in the cave always came to my house with an empty bag when they finished eating rice. My grandfather would ask, "How did you know to find me here?" They answered, "Is there any other person in this town who would do this?" Then, without saying anything, he took an empty bag and filled it with rice and sent it back. Like this, my grandfather always practiced his love for his neighbors. Growing up watching my grandfather, I also am trying to practice love towards my neighbors.

The essential thing in experiencing a miracle of absolute positivity is to train in sharing love. The practice of love is God's greatest joy and the secret to God's great blessing. If you abbreviate every commandment in the Bible in one word, you can say is "love." "Love is the fulfillment of the law." Romans 13:10

Positive energy is charged when love is shared

Love is positive, not negative. A positive person can share love. Also, a negative person can be transformed into a positive person if they practice love. If I love and sacrifice for others, love will definitely become a boomerang and return. "Very truly I tell you, unless a kernel of wheat falls to the ground and dies, it remains only a single seed. But if it dies, it produces many seeds." John 12:24

Austrian psychologist, Dr. Alfred Adler, prescribed depression patients to "make their neighbors happy and give them love," and the patients who followed the prescription had experienced their depression being cured. Depression patients focus only on their inner self and their emotions. If you only think about problems and think about yourself, you can't get out of the pit of depression. But if you share and give love, love and joy returns to me like a boomerang, and depression can be cured.

Yonsei University's Healthy City Research Center takes care of elderly people with depression. One of the many programs for the treatment of depression among the elderly people is a program called, Elderly caring for the Elderly, 'No-No Care.' It's about the elderly who overcame depression and in return help other elderly people dealing with depression. The elderly who attended the treatment program used to make hot pack pockets after the program and deliver them to people in nursing homes. These activities are said to help elderly people suffering from depression improve their self-esteem and instill a sense of self-efficacy. One person who participated in the activity was delighted, saying, "My depression has been relieved and I have received positive energy from life." In addition, an official at the nursing home confessed, "I am so grateful to see the elderly participate in activities in bright colors even in cold weather."

The practice of sharing love was helping others and also served as a treatment for one's depression. This is possible because the positive energy is strongly charged when we make love.

When love is shared you become healthy and happy

When positive energy is charged, people become healthy and happy. Hyung-seok Kim, an honorary professor at Yonsei University, known as the 'philosopher over 100 years old,' explains in an interview that there are two types of people who can never be happy.

The first kind he talks about is a man who doesn't know his spiritual worth. People who pursue money, power, and honor without knowing their spiritual values are difficult to be happy. That's because the more you have, the thirstier and hungrier you get. The second kind are the egotists. A person's character is a vessel for happiness. The egoist's personality is too small to contain happiness. Therefore, the personality of a person who thinks of himself first and lives only for himself cannot be happy because he can never grow.

Sharing love not only makes the person receiving the love happy but also the one sharing it. It heals and strengthens the mind and body of the person who practices sharing. This is because true happiness and health come from sharing and practicing love.

An interesting experiment was conducted with mice at the famous Berkeley University in the U.S. In the first experiment, mice were fed alone and died after 600 days of living. In the second experiment, 5 mice were left to eat together, and they lived 700 days. It increased 100 days. Third, they put a mouse on a person's palm and fed it. When the mouse wanted to eat more, the person feeding the mouse gave more, and when the mouse didn't want to eat, the mouse was fed something else, this mouse lived 950 days. Through these experiments, the research team found that animals who also live with humans in this manner and exchange the power of love, resulting in peace and longer life expectancy. It is important to share love with one another to live happy for a long time,

Gospel is, to know and to share the love of God

Through God's love, we have received eternal life as a gift to live healthy and happy forever. God's blessed news for the world, the good news, or the Gospel, is God's amazing love shown to us through Jesus who died on the cross to save all sinners and was resurrected on the third day. He didn't back down in the face of death and saved us. We didn't love the Lord first. God first loved us and sent Jesus, the son of God.

> *This is love: not that we loved God, but that he loved us and sent his Son as an atoning sacrifice for our sins. _ 1 John 4:10*

The clock in human history is divided into B.C. and A.D. B.C. stands for 'Before Christ, Before Jesus Christ,' and A.D. stands for 'Anno Domini, the Year of the Lord.' The timing is divided based on the birth of Jesus. I think there should be B.C. and A.D. in our lives, as well as in human history. Before knowing Jesus, we were different when we were under the power of sin and death, and after knowing Jesus, who is light and life. A person who has experienced God's love given through the cross, a symbol of absolute positivity, can never live the same life as before. You have to live with a love like Jesus. To love is to resemble Jesus' character the most.

One evening in December 2022, just before Christmas, a man in his 60s collapsed on a road in Gyeyang, Incheon. The people around him walked past him carelessly, but four high school girls who were passing by ran immediately to him. One student calmly performed CPR on the man, who couldn't breathe properly due to convulsions, and friends asked people around him to call 119 for help. As a result of the CPR, he was able to keep the golden time of five minutes, until the ambulance arrived. Thanks to the girls, a man in his 60s was able to survive.

The student who performed CPR is the daughter of a pastor from our church. It's never easy to run to an unfamiliar man and perform CPR without hesitation. But "I couldn't just pass the person who collapsed on the road. It was scary, but I was with my friends, and I was able to practice what I learned in the school health club," the student's words resonated loudly through our society at the time.

When I was in college, I volunteered at Nanjido Village which was full of condemned structures. If you walked for about 30 minutes on the rice fields in Mangwon-dong, there was a large bank in front of Nanjido Island, and a community of people lived around it. About 300 households lived in the neighborhood, where shacks were built with black oil paper, wood, and stones. Adults were working at the construction site, and children were cleaning shoes or picking trash.

At that time, during my volunteer work for about a week, I was shocked and hurt to think that there were people living in such a different environment under the same sky in Seoul. That's when I thought about this, 'Jesus who had died on the cross not only for us but also for them….' Since then, I have imprinted on my mind the idea that those who believe in Jesus should serve these people first.

Evangelism and missions are about sharing love

Evangelism and mission work are about sharing God's love with people. These two are the best for sharing love. My mother also a pastor was dedicated to prayer and evangelism. As soon as she opened her eyes she went out evangelizing all day. When I was a senior in high school, I even told my mother, "Mother, I'm a senior in high school, please pay attention to me." However, with my mother's prayer and devotion to evangelism, I was able to study well and receive great blessings from God. My mother used to preach passionately to young people who were released from prison and would lead them to church. The love of God burned in my mother's heart like fire, so she couldn't do without evangelizing Jeremiah 20:9.

To preach the gospel isn't just about shouting, "Believe in Jesus." Those who have experienced God's love through the gospel share the love they've received. At those moments, the gospel is passed down. The Apostle John said that when we share love, people in the world will see the invisible God.

Dear friends, since God so loved us, we also ought to love one another. No one has ever seen God; but if we love one another, God lives in us and his love is made complete in us. _ 1 John 4:11-12

Ever since I became the senior pastor of Yoido Full Gospel Church, I have continuously practiced various ways to share love. Every year, one-third of the church's budget is spent on sharing love. Visiting a small village with subdivided rooms to comfort those in need, sharing 'hope box of love' and 'kimjang kimchi of love' for underprivileged neighbors, free procedures for heart disease patients, support for multi-children families, assisting North Korean defectors, are some of the ways we share the love. We have been actively carrying out projects to provide subsidies for young people and the elderlies in need.

Through sharing love, people in the world may not pay attention to us, but they will see Jesus who saved us because Jesus showed us the biggest example of love.

Bulk up your love muscles

One of the trainings that God gave the people of Israel was the 'training of giving.' God first made the people of Israel offer the first fruit of all the crops Exodus 23:19. We are to give God what is most precious, not what is left after use. He also trained the people to help their poor neighbors. For example, the owner of the vineyard did not harvest all the grapes, but left some for the traveler or the widow, and not all the ears of grain were harvested, leaving some behind Leviticus 19:9-10. People in the world judge others by how much they have but God's judgment is different. God sees how much we have given and how much we've shared with what we have.

There is a deacon I met while I was a pastor in training. He was a successful businessman, and many people around him have made financial requests but the deacon didn't lend money to anyone. The deacon explained his reason. "I once lent money to a close friend and didn't receive it back. It always hurt me because I lost money and my friend. So after that, when someone in need comes, I check if the situation is really bad and just help them without any conditions. And then I forget the fact that I helped."

I was particularly impressed by the deacon's words, 'I forget about it after I give help.' People in the world are very calculative. If you give something, you calculate what you'll definitely get back. Therefore, it is not given at all to those who are incapable of repaying it. But Jesus said that giving is better than receiving Acts 20:35. The Bible also says that giving to a person in need without calculating what he will receive is the secret to receiving God's blessing.

> *So that the Levites (who have no allotment or inheritance of their own) and the foreigners, the fatherless and the widows who live in your towns may come and eat and be satisfied, and so that the LORD your God may bless you in all the work of your hands. _ Deuteronomy 14:29*

> *Whoever is kind to the poor lends to the LORD, and he will reward them for what they have done. _ Proverbs 19:17*

> *Give, and it will be given to you. A good measure, pressed down, shaken together and running over, will be poured into your lap. For with the measure you use, it will be measured to you. _ Luke 6:38*

Pastor Rick Warren says that if you don't do muscle exercises, you'll lose them. If you don't use the muscles of love given by God, muscles weaken and decline. Just as athletes train and prepare for the Olympics, we should always train and prepare for love and service. This love training will be a great blessing in this life and in the future1 Timothy 4:8.

Be attentive to the needs of others

To share love well, it is important to have sensitivity to people's needs. Jesus was always sensitive to people's needs. Chapter 8 of the Gospel of Mark shows how sensitive Jesus was to people's needs. When the crowd who listened and followed Jesus faced difficulty because they had nothing to eat, Jesus said, "I have compassion for these people; they have already been with me three days and have nothing to eat. If I send them home hungry, they will collapse on the way, because some of them have come a long distance."Mark 8:2-3 In response to Jesus' words, the disciples only replied, "Where in this remote place can anyone get enough bread to feed them?"Mark 8:4 But Jesus fed the 4,000 people who gathered there with five loaves of bread and two small fish. Jesus always knew people's needs and was the one who filled them.

In Chapter 9 of the Book of Acts, there was a woman named Tabitha, Dorcas, who did good deeds and gave relief. She showed kindness by distributing handmade clothes to the poor. She fell ill and died, and as Peter, the Apostle was passing through Joppa, was invited to Tabitha's house. All the widows gathered in the room and mourned with tears for her, she loved to serve and help others. Then Peter knelt down and prayed, and when he commanded the body, "Tabitha, get up!" she came back to life. The miracle of Tabitha's life, who had died, but was raised to life by the power of love that she filled people's needs with. How do you think Tabitha lived after she came back to life? Perhaps she gave love by sharing the gospel of Jesus and filling the needs of others as before.

To practice love, like Jesus, we must always look to see what people need. We must distinguish whether the need is physical, material, emotional, or spiritual, and seek God's wisdom and supply to fill it. If you have a heart of true love and compassion, God the Holy Spirit will also teach you how to practice love.

Life of sharing even the smallest things

I was impressed by the article of Deacon Byung-rok Kim, a shoe repairman. The deacon, who has been repairing shoes since 1996, suddenly thought, "How many old shoes does each family leave unworn?" So he put a sign in front of his store, saying, "If there are shoes you don't wear or want to throw away shoes, please bring them to the shoe hospital." After that, about 5,000 pairs of shoes were collected, repaired, and distributed to neighbors in need. Deacon Kim's good deeds did not end here. He went to a nursing home to volunteer for haircuts and lived helping underprivileged children, boys and girls, and retired pastors. In addition, he sold 700 million KRW worth of land he bought with retirement funds in 2020 and donated it to those who have been struggling due to COVID-19.

Later, Deacon Kim said in an interview, "Christians like me have gained new life through Jesus, so the life they live is a bonus. So there's nothing to be greedy about. I'll give it all away before I go." Looking at Deacon Byung-rok Kim's faith, you can feel that the spirit of love for our neighbors residing in true faith. We are all living our lives as a bonus because of Jesus we have new life. Sharing love is the way to give back some of the grace our Lord has given to us as He has given us new life.

We must give thanks to God for what he has given us and we must now live by sharing the things God has given us. A person with material things can give material things. When John the Baptist came and preached a spiritual sermon to bear fruit worthy of repentance, people asked what they were to do. Then John said, "Anyone who has two shirts should share with the one who has none, and anyone who has food should do the same." Luke 3:11 There is also a saying in our country that "the storehouse is generous." Buying a meal and sharing what we have should continue in our lives.

If you look at the *Beautiful Sharing Class* written by Sung-sil Jeon, you can see that there are various ways you can share love. We usually think that we have to do something very big to help and serve someone but sharing love can start with small things.

Japan's social enterprise 'Table for Two' has started a campaign to donate about 200 won or 20 yen since 2007. When you have lunch, you can choose a diet meal that subtracts 20 yen and with this money, you can help starving children in other countries.

Sharing love doesn't just mean sharing material things. We can share our talents and our time. If we study more than others and have knowledge, we can share that knowledge. It is also necessary to share our interests and minds. In particular, it is very important to listen to such people's stories and understand their minds in situations as many people are suffering from mental illness these days.

Jeon says, citing the 2007 shooting at Virginia Tech in the United States, "Psychologists say that if he had at least one friend who could share his feelings, the shooting would not have happened, if he had a friend who understood his mind." Approaching someone, comforting them, and giving words of encouragement can also be a way of sharing love.

We can also share spiritual things. You can use the gift of the Holy Spirit you received to serve the church and the church members. Those who have received the grace of intercessory prayer may pray for the church and the pastor, for the back sliding church members, for the evangelist, for the nation and the people. Those who have received the gift of encouragement can console and encourage those who are in sorrowRomans 12:8. Everything we have can be a tool for sharing love.

God is love. Whoever lives in love lives in God, and God in them.
_ 1 John 4:16

The biggest miracle of our lives is that God saved us and loves us. The love we received from God is so immense and amazing that we have no choice but to live with gratitude every day. Whenever I see the cross of Jesus Christ, I realize the hope and love of absolute positivity. Also, God's absolute love for us, no creature or obstacle can separateRomans 8:35-39. Therefore, we must live with faith of absolute positivity in God. No matter what difficulties you face in your life, God works together for the good. Now, with the holy dream that God gives you, be a comissioned with Christ declaring with words of faith, giving thanks, and sharing love. I hope the principle of absolute positivity will bring upon incredible changes, blessings, and miracles in your life.

Examples of proclamation of sharing love

The next declaration is an example. Make a declaration that suits you. Declare "with the heart of Jesus' love."

- I love God more than anything else!
- I value myself and love myself!
- I respect and love everyone I meet!
- I value what I do and I love it!
- I will realize God's love is bigger through hardships and problems!
- I cherish, pray and love our church and our pastors!
- I look forward to my future and believe that good things will happen!
- I'll help the poor with some of the things I have!
- I will serve the church and others with the talents or gifts I have!
- I will approach someone who needs prayer or encouragement or help and assist them!

Positivity Quotient Check List ☑

Sharing Love Quotient Check List?

Instructions: Please read each statement and select the most appropriate response to indicate how frequently you experience the behavior described in the statement.

Statements	Never	Rarely	Some times	Often	Always
	1	2	3	4	5
1. Knowing and sharing God's love is one of the core values of my life.					
2. I tend to look at the needs of the people I meet.					
3. If my neighbor or friend is in trouble, I am willing to help.					
4. I pray for family and friends who don't know the gospel.					
5. I use my gifts and talents to help the church and my neighbors.					
6. I preach the gospel to my neighbors and colleagues who don't believe in God.					
7. I participate in helping the poor in need.					
8. I pray for and comfort my neighbors who are ill or have problems.					
9. I share and help with programs in the church or community. I participate in campaigns such as blood drives, fundraising for relief, etc.					
10. I practice kindness and love without expecting anything in return.					

After reading each statement, check the corresponding box.
Add up the checked scores for each statement.

Totals (   ) points

The Miracle of
Absolute Positivity

Appendix

Absolute Positivity Index (PQ Check List)

Positivity Quotient Check List

Positive Attitude Quotient Check List?

Instructions: Please read each statement and select the most appropriate response to indicate how frequently you experience the behavior described in the statement.

Statements	Never	Rarely	Some times	Often	Always
	1	2	3	4	5
1. When stressed, I think positively and overcome it.					
2. Negative emotions don't determine the attitude or direction of life.					
3. After experiencing hardship and difficulty, I learn from them and get back up.					
4. I usually believe in the power of positivity and am very conscious about it.					
5. I have high expectations of my remaining life and future.					
6. When looking at the environment or people, I try to see the brighter side than the darker.					
7. I visualize myself doing well or succeeding.					
8. There are more people who say positive things around me than negative things.					
9. I don't think I'm going to fail at something before I start it.					
10. I have a lot of love and positive energy in me.					

After reading each statement, check the corresponding box.
Add up the checked scores for each statement.

Totals (   )points

Positivity Quotient Check List ☑

Positive Faith Quotient Check List?

Instructions: Please read each statement and select the most appropriate response to indicate how frequently you experience the behavior described in the statement.

Statements	Never	Rarely	Some times	Often	Always
	1	2	3	4	5
1. God is the most important person in my life and I believe I love Him the most.					
2. I believe God is with me when I pray.					
3. I believe the cross of Jesus Christ displays the love of God's absolute positivity.					
4. No matter what hardship and difficulty, I am not discouraged because God is present.					
5. I engage with God and talk to Him daily.					
6. When what I want isn't quickly achieved, I think and wait, "There will be God's timing."					
7. In my faith life, I experience and am greatly moved by God's love.					
8. When I pray, I often experience despair and negative thoughts disappearing.					
9. I read and meditate on God's Word daily.					
10. I believe that whether you're good, evil, at peace or struggling, it's all under God's sovereignty.					

After reading each statement, check the corresponding box.
Add up the checked scores for each statement.

Totals (　　　　　　)points

Positivity Quotient Check List

Positive View of Myself Quotient Check List?

Instructions: Please read each statement and select the most appropriate response to indicate how frequently you experience the behavior described in the statement.

Statements	Never	Rarely	Some times	Often	Always
	1	2	3	4	5
1. I think I'm attractive.					
2. I don't compare myself with others and feel inferior.					
3. I believe that God made me unique and precious.					
4. I think I have enough qualifications to be loved.					
5. I feel happy now.					
6. I am not swayed by people's gossip or criticism.					
7. I believe that I have talent and value.					
8. I value and love myself.					
9. I think I can do well with whatever I'm entrusted with.					
10. I picture my future self as I declare and bless my future.					

After reading each statement, check the corresponding box.
Add up the checked scores for each statement.

Totals (   )points

Positivity Quotient Check List ☑

Positive View of Others Quotient Check List?

Instructions: Please read each statement and select the most appropriate response to indicate how frequently you experience the behavior described in the statement.

Statements	Never	Rarely	Some times	Often	Always
	1	2	3	4	5
1. When I see others, I try to see their strengths than their weaknesses.					
2. It isn't difficult to talk with someone who thinks differently than me.					
3. I'm happy to help someone in a difficult situation.					
4. I consider other people's feelings and value them.					
5. When treating others, I don't lose my smile and friendliness.					
6. I cherish the people I meet and bless them.					
7. If it's for someone else, I can take a loss.					
8. I can be friendly to people who misunderstand and hate me.					
9. I tend to encourage and praise people.					
10. I can forgive the person who hurt me or gave me a difficult time.					

After reading each statement, check the corresponding box.
Add up the checked scores for each statement.

Totals (　　　　　)points

Positivity Quotient Check List ☑

Positive View of Work and Calling Quotient Check List?

Instructions: Please read each statement and select the most appropriate response to indicate how frequently you experience the behavior described in the statement.

Statements	Never	Rarely	Some times	Often	Always
	1	2	3	4	5
1. I am enjoying what I'm doing.					
2. I think the work I'm doing is God's mission.					
3. When faced with a difficulty, rather than giving up, I rise to the challenge.					
4. I often think of ideas while I'm working.					
5. I pray to God before I go to work and pray while I work.					
6. When I work, I am kind and considerate of the people around me.					
7. I work with passion.					
8. I do my best in everything I'm entrusted with.					
9. I don't think there is work or my mission has ended because I have aged.					
10. To get better at work, I manage my physical strength.					

After reading each statement, check the corresponding box.
Add up the checked scores for each statement.

Totals (　　　　　　)points

Positivity Quotient Check List ☑

Positive View of Environment Quotient Check List?

Instructions: Please read each statement and select the most appropriate response to indicate how frequently you experience the behavior described in the statement.

Statements	Never	Rarely	Some times	Often	Always
	1	2	3	4	5
1. I don't complain when problems arise.					
2. I don't dwell on past wounds and torment myself.					
3. I believe everything that happens to me and my environment is in God's providence.					
4. I often remember the grace God gave me and gain strength.					
5. I believe God will work together for the good even in difficult situations.					
6. I tend to think positively about the community I belong to.					
7. I pray for and love the church I attend.					
8. I cherish and value my company.					
9. I don't criticize people in my community.					
10. I always have a positive attitude when I'm with or working with people.					

After reading each statement, check the corresponding box.
Add up the checked scores for each statement.

Totals (　　　　　)points

Positivity Quotient Check List

Positive View of Future Quotient Check List?

Instructions: Please read each statement and select the most appropriate response to indicate how frequently you experience the behavior described in the statement.

Statements	Never	Rarely	Some times	Often	Always
	1	2	3	4	5
1. I believe that God has great expectations and plans for my life.					
2. I feel optimistic and hopeful about my future.					
3. I'm expecting God to give me a miracle in my life.					
4. When I pray in the Holy Spirit, I feel my holy desires will come true.					
5. The vision and dream that God gives me is passionately enflamed in my heart.					
6. When hardship comes my way, I persevere with the dream, the friend that God has given me.					
7. I always picture achieving my vision and my future.					
8. I write down my dream and pray specifically to achieve it.					
9. I am always studying and learning to achieve my dream.					
10. I am a missionary to fulfill God's dream and vision until I die.					

After reading each statement, check the corresponding box.
Add up the checked scores for each statement.

Totals (   )points

Positivity Quotient Check List ☑

Proclamation of Positive Words Quotient Check List?

Instructions: Please read each statement and select the most appropriate response to indicate how frequently you experience the behavior described in the statement.

Statements	Never	Rarely	Some times	Often	Always
	1	2	3	4	5
1. Negative words never come out of my mouth.					
2. I often say words of encouragement and praise to others.					
3. I think positively of myself. I bless and declare.					
4. I believe that unbelief and negative words can distract from God's work and miracles.					
5. I often say words of blessings to others.					
6. I always read and meditate on God's Word.					
7. I pray by reciting the Word of God using it in appropriate situations.					
8. I give hope and words of life to others.					
9. I record God's vision and declare it whenever I have time.					
10. I believe there is power in words of faith. I declare and command diseases and problems to be healed and solved.					

After reading each statement, check the corresponding box.
Add up the checked scores for each statement.

Totals (   )points

Positivity Quotient Check List ☑

Absolute Gratitude Quotient Check List?

Instructions: Please read each statement and select the most appropriate response to indicate how frequently you experience the behavior described in the statement.

Statements	Never	Rarely	Some times	Often	Always
	1	2	3	4	5
1. I confess my gratitude to God when I wake up in the morning.					
2. I look for something to be thankful for even the smallest things in my daily life.					
3. I often express my gratitude to people around me.					
4. I am grateful and pray even if there is no immediate response to my prayer.					
5. I confess my gratitude rather than my complaints even if something difficult happens.					
6. I don't complain about what I don't have, but rather, give thanks for what I do have.					
7. I meditate on God's grace by writing in my thank you journal every day.					
8. I believe that hardships and problems are opportunities for faith and growth of character. I give thanks.					
9. I believe that God will make things for good even if things don't go the way I planned. I give thanks.					
10. I end each day with a prayer of thanksgiving before going to bed.					

After reading each statement, check the corresponding box.
Add up the checked scores for each statement.

Totals (   )points

Positivity Quotient Check List

Sharing Love Quotient Check List?

Instructions: Please read each statement and select the most appropriate response to indicate how frequently you experience the behavior described in the statement.

Statements	Never	Rarely	Some times	Often	Always
	1	2	3	4	5
1. Knowing and sharing God's love is one of the core values of my life.					
2. I tend to look at the needs of the people I meet.					
3. If my neighbor or friend is in trouble, I am willing to help.					
4. I pray for family and friends who don't know the gospel.					
5. I use my gifts and talents to help the church and my neighbors.					
6. I preach the gospel to my neighbors and colleagues who don't believe in God.					
7. I participate in helping the poor in need.					
8. I pray for and comfort my neighbors who are ill or have problems.					
9. I share and help with programs in the church or community. I participate in campaigns such as blood drives, fundraising for relief, etc.					
10. I practice kindness and love without expecting anything in return.					

After reading each statement, check the corresponding box.
Add up the checked scores for each statement.

Totals (　　　　　)points

Absolute Positivity Index(PQ)
Measurement and Evaluation

The Positivity Quotient(PQ) is the most important asset in life. PQ is a great force beyond IQ, environment, and destiny. The higher the PQ, the more amazing changes and miracles you'll experience in your life.

Welcome to the PQ Checklist Evaluation after reading this book. This is the time to measure and evaluate the Positive Index presented at the end of each chapter. Let's proceed in the following order.

1. Write down the Absolute Positivity Index scores of the 10 areas and add them up

* 50 points for each section. 500 points for 10 items.

no	Area	Total
1	Positive Attitude Quotient Check List	pts
2	Positive Faith Quotient Check List	pts
3	Positive View of Myself Quotient Check List	pts
4	Positive View of Others Quotient Check List	pts
5	Positive View of Work and Calling Quotient Check List	pts
6	Positive View of Environment Quotient Check List	pts
7	Positive View of Future Quotient Check List	pts
8	Proclamation of Positive Words Quotient Check List	pts
9	Absolute Gratitude Quotient Check List	pts
10	Sharing Love Quotient Check List	pts
Total		**pts**

2. Divide the total score by 5.(100pt conversion basis)

* **e.g.** | If your total score is 400, your score is 80 (400÷5=80).

Record your own score. (   ) pts

---

3. Find out your PQ (100pt conversion basis) level.

90~100pts	Your PQ level is Excellent. You are a very positive person.
	Having absolute positive energy, you can be happy and successful in whatever you do. Look forward to amazing miracles that will appear throughout your life.
80~89pts	Your PQ level is Above Average. You are a positive person.
	You have a high level of positive energy. If you use this energy, you can have great success. Make up for the shortcomings and move towards excellence.
60~79pts	Your PQ level is Average. You have a lot of positives.
	You have a lot of positive assets. Out of the 10 areas, which part were you most vulnerable? If you follow the guidance of the Holy Spirit, you can make up for the deficiencies. You can be the owner of absolute positive energy.
40~59pts	Your PQ level is Below Average. There's a fight between positivity & negativity in you.
	You need to take better care of your mind and thoughts. Please socialize with positive people and habituate absolute positive thoughts, declarations, and activities. There will be a big change.
39pts~below	Your PQ level is Low. Unfortunately, your negativity index is higher.
	A big effort is needed for the positive index but don't be disappointed. You have a God of absolute positivity. With intensive counseling and training, you can be a positive person too.

References

- Joo-hwan Kim, 『Resilience』 Seoul: Wisdom House, 2019.
- Hyung-seok Kim, 『Kim Hyung-seok's Life Question and Answer』, Seoul: Miryu Bookstore, 2022.
- Nick Vučić, 『Nick Vučić's hug』, Jong-hoon Choi, Seoul: Durano, 2010.
- Deborah Norville, 『The power of appreciation』, Tae-joon Yoon, Seoul: Wisdom House, 2008.
- David Soffer, 『God Is Inescapable』, London: Westminster Press, 1959.
- Laurent Gunnell, 『Go the way you want』, Yong-nam Kim, Paju: a harmonious life, 2009.
- Max Lucado 『Pastor, it's hard to live』, Myung-sook Park, Paju: Poiema, 2013.
- Esther Park, a disease that takes care of sick people want to be Pastor Won, Beautiful Companion, 2011.
- Ben Carson, 『God-given hand』, Sung-ok Eom, Seoul: Eun-sung, 1999.
- Sonia Lyubomusky, 『How to be happy: need to practice happiness』, Hye-kyung Oh, Seoul: Knowledge Nomad, 2007.
- Adam Grant, 『Give and Take』, Tae-joon Yoon, Seoul: Thinking Research Institute, 2013.
- Albert Bandura, 『Self-efficacy and quality of life』 Young-shin Park, Seoul: History of educational science, 2001.
- Edward Bounds, 『The heart of prayer』, Yong-bok Lee, Seoul: Kyujang, 2007.
- Erich Fromm, 『The Art of Love』, Moon-soo Hwang, Seoul: Literary Publishing House, 2019.
- Wei Shueying, 『Harvard 4:30 a.m. 』, Jung-eun Lee, Seoul: Rice Maker, 2017.
- William Barclay, 『Secret to Satisfaction』, Sung-taek Kang, Seoul: a history of reformist theology, 2012.
- Young-eun Yoon, 『Positive overwhelms Passion』, Seoul: Prenemy, 2021
- Mi-young Lee, Man-seok Kim, Byung-wook Kim, 『Management is fun when you meet Gatitude』, Goyang: Provence, 2014.
- Younghoon Lee, 『Miracle of Appreciation』, Seoul: Durano, 2013.

■ Younghoon Lee, 『Gratitude QT 365』, Seoul: Seoul Speech History, 2022.
■ Younghoon Lee, 『Only by the Holy Spirit』, Seoul: Institute for Church Growth, 2022.
■ Younghoon Lee, 『12 Wisdoms to Success: Seoul』, Institute for Church Growth, 2023
■ Ji-sun Lee, 『Pretty Good Happy Ending』, Paju: Munhakdongne, 2022.
■ Yong-jin Jang, 『The communication of a good worker』, Seoul: Sam&Parkers, 2008.
■ Sung-sil Jeon, 『Beautiful Sharing Class』, Seoul: Good Book Store, 2012.
■ Yong-gi Cho, 『4th Dimensional Spirituality』, Seoul: Institute for Church Growth, 2010.
■ Yong-gi Cho, 『Heart Sky』, Seoul: Institute fpr Church Growth, 2009
■ John Gattman, 『Science of Love』, Young-jo Seo, Seoul: Han Hae-rim, 2018
■ John Gordon, 『Energy Bus』, Young-man Yoo, Soo-kyung Lee, Seoul: Sam&Parkers, 2019.
■ John Powell, 『The season of the heart』, Hong-kyu Jung, Seoul: Paul Daughter, 1992.
■ Charles Duhig, 『The power of habit』, Joo-heon Kang, Paju: Gallion, 2012.
■ Kwang-kyu Choi, 『God on everything』, Seoul: Compass, 2014.
■ Kelly Choi, 『WEALTHINKING』, Seoul: Dasan Books, 2021.
■ Thomas Stanley, 『Millionaire mind』, Seok-hoon Jang, Seoul: Bookhouse, 2007.
■ Tom Peters, 『Tom Peters Excellent Business Conditions』, Mi-jung Kim, Seoul: Korea Economic Daily, 2022.
■ Fred Pollack, 『The Image of the Future』, Amsterdam: Elsevier Scientific Publishing Company, 1973.
■ A. W. Tozer, 『Be Nailed to the cross』, Yong-bok Lee, Seoul: Kyujang, 2015.
■ Lisa Hilton, 『Positivity+: How You Can Add More Happiness to Your Life』, Independently published, 2023.
■ Shawn Achor, 『The Happiness Advantage: How a Positive Brain Fuels Success in Work and Life』, Currency; Illustrated edition, 2018.
■ Whitney Goodman, 『Toxic Positivity: Keeping It Real in a World Obsessed with Being Happy』, TarcherPerigee, 2022.

The Miracle of Absolute Positivity

The Miracle of Absolute Positivity

The Miracle of Absolute Positivity

Published by CGW(Church Growth Worldwide)
CGW(Church Growth Worldwide) holds the exclusive publishing rights for both the Korean and English editions of this book.

- Address: 59, Eunhaeng-ro, Yeongdeungpo-gu, Seoul, Korea
- E-mail: icg7936@pastor21.net

Exclusive U.S. Distribution and Sales by LOGOS USA
LOGOS USA holds exclusive rights to distribute and sell this book in the U.S. publishing market. For any inquiries regarding purchases, please contact LOGOS USA.

- Address: 3268 Smithtown Road, Suwanee, GA 30024, USA
- E-mail: logosusainc@gmail.com
- Phone: +1 770-945-4447

ISBN 978-89-8304-364-1(03230)